Survival Guide

Earlene Festervan

ACA
FOUNDED 1870
American Correctional Association
Lanham, Maryland

Printed in the United States of America by Graphic Communications,
Upper Malboro, Maryland
For information on publications and videos available from ACA,
contact our worldwide web home page at:
http://www.corrections.com/aca

ISBN -156991-128-2

This publication may be ordered from:
American Correctional Association
4380 Forbes Boulevard
Lanham, Maryland 20706-4322
1-800-222-5646, ext. 1859

Library of Congress Cataloging-in-Publication Data
Festervan, Earlene
        Survival guide for new probation officers/ Earlene Festervan.
                p. cm.
        Includes bibliographical references.
        ISBN 1-56991-128-2 (pbk.)
            1. Probation–United States.
            2. Probation officers–United States
        I. Title.
HV9304 .F47 2000
364.6'3'0973–dc21   00-044808

CONTENTS

This book is dedicated to the memory of Charles W. Hawkes, "The Chief" from 1964-1988.

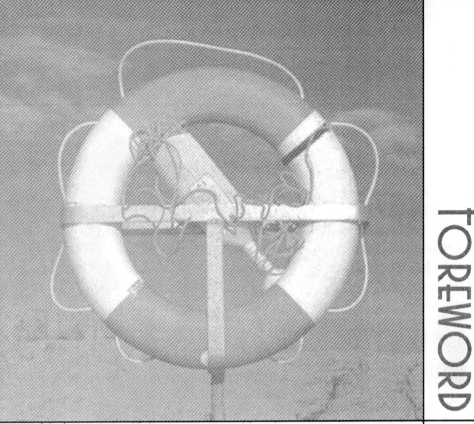

Despite the growing number of individuals in prisons and jails, the vast majority of offenders in this country are supervised in the community. Probation is an important and cost-effective alternative to incarceration that is often used by judges. When administered with proper case management and accountability consistent with recognized correctional standards, probation provides useful services for enhancing social order and public safety. Ultimately, the success of probation as a sentencing alternative is up to the individual offender. However, success also is tied closely with the performance of the probation officer.

In *Survival Guide for New Probation Officers*, Earlene Festervan offers valuable guidance to help people new to the job become successful probation officers. Drawing on her experience as an officer, Festervan addresses a wide range of probation concerns, from day-to-day interaction with the courts and police, to some of the long-term challenges of the profession, such as stress and political controversy. She covers the practical details that every probation officer needs to know, including office etiquette, ethical considerations, time management, and safety in the field and in the office.

This book will assist new probation officers in becoming better probation officers. It can be useful in making probation services more effective. Students of criminal justice who are considering a career in probation also will benefit from this book. It offers a realistic view of what the job requires, and provides practical advice on how to meet those requirements.

James A. Gondles, Jr., CAE
Executive Director
American Correctional Association

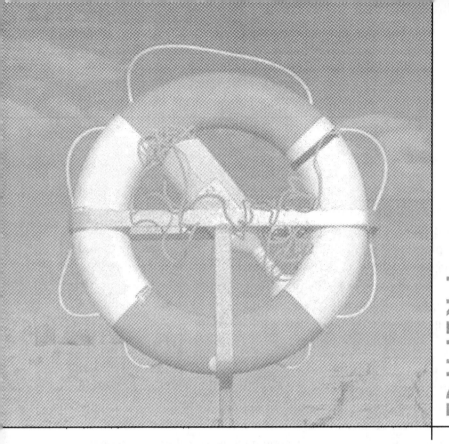

It was my good fortune to begin my probation career in an excellent department where the chief and his subordinates held truth, honor, and service as the most elementary principles. We were expected to be the best probation officers in the state, so we tried, and often succeeded.

Because I was hired for a new caseload that had not yet been developed, I had the unique opportunity to spend almost a month with an experienced officer, Lisa Spaulding. From her and from my supervisor, Steve Corley, I learned the history and philosophy of my department. They taught me the chief's philosophy that we are public servants and we are accountable to the public and our clients. They showed me the ins and outs of casework, court work, and involvement with the police and other agencies. They passed along a sense of pride and dedication that has lasted me for more than sixteen years in this field.

When I transferred to another jurisdiction some years later, I realized just how fortunate I had been. In most departments, there is little time for the training and development of new officers. As a supervisor, I have come to know how crucial this initial training is and long to be able to provide it. This book is an effort to fill a void for both new and experienced officers and to reach students aspiring to a career in probation. I do not presume to contradict or replace any training or procedures provided by probation departments or academies. Instead, I hope this work will be a happy supplement to the training already in place across the country. I am writing from the setting I know, which is probation; however, parole officers and caseworkers in other human service agencies can use much of this information.

In other circumstances, I could have been the offender sitting across the desk from you. Many officers can say the same. I believe it is important for us to remember that although we are authority figures, we are not above the law or better than other people. We are, however, more accountable than other people. This is a service business. Individuals should be here only if they have a genuine love for others and a desire to help others. I am grateful for a good job and the opportunity to make a difference. I am thankful for the personal growth and change I have experienced as a result of my profession.

I want to thank Alice Fins from the American Correctional Association for her kind assistance and encouragement; Karen Fuller from the American Probation and Parole Association for research assistance; Ed Read, Supervising U.S. Probation Officer in Washington D.C.; Ken Cater, Deputy Commissioner of the California Board of Prison Terms and former Chief Probation Officer in El Dorado County, California; Terry Berg, U.S. Department of Justice/Criminal Division/ Computer Crimes and Intellectual Property Section; and the members of the National Association of Probation Executives who graciously answered questions and provided input.

I am very grateful to the Texas gang: Jan Watts, my friend, fellow officer and illustrator; Dan Beto, Correctional Management Institute of Texas; Montie Morgan, Director, Jefferson County Community Supervision and Corrections; James "Bubba" Martin, Chief Juvenile

Probation Officer, Jefferson County; Kathy Welch, Deputy Director, Jefferson County Juvenile Probation; the staff at Jefferson County Restitution Center No. 1, especially James Alamo, Donna Kountz, and Judy Williams for their computer expertise and advice; Jimmie Adams, LPC; Michael Fairley, Jefferson County Community Supervision and Corrections ISP Supervisor; and especially, the world's best boss, Clay Childress, Associate Director for Residential Services, Jefferson County Community Supervision and Corrections. Finally, thanks to Jamie Venable for his unwavering support and belief in me, no matter what.

Good reading and good luck.

Probation As a Profession

Probation is a widely misunderstood term and concept in our society. Lay people use the terms probation and parole interchangeably, and even other criminal justice personnel may not understand the mission and duties of a probation officer. To clarify some of the confusion, let us begin with the definition of probation. Probation is the conditional release of an individual by the court after the offender has been found guilty of a crime and before sentencing to prison.

Probation may be administered by the courts as part of the judicial system, by the executive branch of government as an administrative function, or administered by private agencies contracting with the courts or executive agencies as shown in Table 1.1. In some jurisdictions, probation and parole are combined in a centralized state agency; in other locales, each is a separate entity. Some officers work both juvenile and adult probation cases; others are employed in separate departments or units. Regardless of how a probation department is administered, the essential functions are similar. A probation officer working for a court in one state will be charged with many of the same duties as an officer working for the corrections department under a gubernatorial appointee in another state. These common duties and characteristics are due in part to the historical and philosophical background of the profession.

Table 1.1   Probation Providers

as of September 30, 1997

State	Adult Probation Services	Juvenile Probation Services
AL	Bd Pardons & Paroles	Dept Youth Svs ($# only) & Co Cts
AK	Dept Corrections	DHSS/Div Family & Youth Svcs*
AZ	State Courts	States Courts
AR	Bd C&Cmty Pun/Dept Cmty Pun*	Courts/DHS/Youth Svcs Bd
CA	Co Courts	Co Courts
CO	Judicial Dept	Judicial Dept
CT	Office Adult prob	Superior Court Juv Matters/Family Div
DE	DOC/Div Cmty Svcs	DSCYF/Div Youth Rehab/Cmty Svcs*
DC	DC Superior Ct/Social Svcs Div	DC Superior Ct/Social Svcs Div
FL	DOC/Prob & Parole Svcs*	DHRS/Juvenile Justice
GA	DOC/Cmty Corr Div	DHR/Dept Ch Youth Svcs & Co Courts
HI	State Judiciary/Prob Ofc	State Judiciary/Family Courts
ID	DOC/Div Field & Cmty Svcs	DHW/Bur of Juv Justice/Co Courts
IL	Judicial Circuits/Prob Div	Judicial Circuits/Prob Div
IN	Judicial/County Courts	Judicial/County Courts
IA	DOC/Div Cmty Corr Svcs	Judicial Districts
KS	Judicial Districts/Ct Svcs Div	Judicial Districts/Ct Svcs Div
KY	DOC/Cmty Svcs & Facil/Div PP	Dept Juvenile Justice
LA	DPSC/Div Prob & Parole*	DPSC/Ofc Youth Development
ME	DOC/Div Prob & Parole	DOC/Div Prob & Parole
MD	DPSCS/Div Parole & Prob	Dept Juv Svcs
MA	Office of Cmsnr Prob/Courts	Office of Cmsnr of Prob/Courts
MI	DOC/Field Op Admin & Dist Cts	DSS/Office Delinq Svcs/Co Cts
MN	DOC/Prob Par Supv Rel*/Co Cts or CCA	DOC/Prob Par Supv Rel*/Co Cts or CCA
MS	DOC/Cmty Svcs Div	DHS/DYS/Cmty Svcs Div
MO	DOC/Bd Prob & Parole	Judicial Circuits
MT	DCHS/CD/Prob & Parole Bureau	Judicial Districts
NE	NE Prob System	NE Prob System
NV	DMV/Div Parole & Prob	District Courts
NH	DOC/Div Field Svcs*	DHHS/DCYS/Bur Children
NJ	The Judiciary/Prob Div	DLPS/Juvenile Justice Cmsn
NM	CD/Prob & Parole Div*	CYFD/Cmty Svcs Div
NY	Div Prob & Corr Alt/Co Courts	Exec Dept/Div Prob & Corr Alt/Courts
NC	DOC/Div Adult Prob & Parole	Admin Office Courts/Juv Svcs Div
ND	DCR/Div Parole & Prob	DCR/Div Juv Svcs*/Supr Cts
OH	DRC/Prob & Parole Field Svcs*	Co Court
OK	DOC/Prob & Parole Svcs*	DHS/OHH/Juvenile Svcs Unit*
OR	DOC/Cmty Corrections	OR Youth Authority
PA	Bd of Prob & Parole* & Co Cts	Co Courts
RI	DOC/Div Rehab Svcs	DCYF/Div Juv Corr Svcs
SC	Dept Prob, Parole &, Prdn Svcs	Dept Juv Justice/Cmty Div
SD	Unified Judicial Sys/Ct Svcs Dept	Unified Judicial Sys/Ct Svcs Dept
TN	DOC/Adult Field Svcs*	DCS/Juv Corr Div*
TX	TDCJ/Cmty Jus Asist Div/Dist Cts	Co Courts
UT	DOC/Div Field Operations	Juv Courts
VT	AHS/DOC	DSRS/Div Social Svcs
VA	DOC/Div Cmty Corr	Dept Youth & Fam Svcs*
WA	DOC/Div Cmty Corr & Co Cts	Co Courts
WV	DPS/DOC & Judicial Circuits	DMAPS/DJS (Compact), Jud Circuits**
WI	DOC/Div Prob & Parole	Co Social Svcs Depts
WY	DOC/Div Field Services	Dept Family Svcs/Co Munic Depts
US	Admin Ofc of US Courts/Div of Prob	

Notes:
*   Accredited by Commission on Accreditation for Corrections.
** WV—Under state statute, juv release is judicially, rather than administratively, determined and is considered probation.
The following states have one or more independent county, municipal or city departments: CO, GA, IN, KS, KY, LA, MO, NE, NY, OK, TN, WY.
All Boards are independent except MD, MI, MN, OH, TX.

HISTORY OF PROBATION

Probation as a practice derives from the concept of mercy, which is as old as humankind. The Old Testament describes "Cities of Refuge" where individuals could go if they had killed another unintentionally. In the fourteenth century, English Common Law provided for the suspension of sentences in certain cases, but it is in the United States where the term *probation* probably originated. John Augustus, the father of probation, practiced probation as a volunteer officer as early as 1841. He provided services for first-time offenders or those who had committed minor offenses, finding them jobs, helping then with living arrangements, and vouching for them that they would not reoffend. By 1878, Massachusetts had hired the first paid officers in the country, and by 1899, Chicago followed suit by establishing a juvenile court and probation department (Cohn, 1994).

Casework was the standard for these early probation officers, who, with their roots in the social work discipline, emphasized the rehabilitation and reclamation of the offender. Social work theory dominated the field for many years, but eventually probation evolved into a more punitive or law-enforcement mind-set. The reasons for this are many, but they include the declining number of qualified caseworkers who entered the profession, political concerns reflecting the public's fear of crime, the increase of drug abuse and violent crime, and prison crowding, which caused the release of more dangerous offenders to probation.

MODERN DAY PROBATION

According to the Bureau of Justice Statistics (August, 1999), there are more than four million people on probation or parole in the United States; of this figure, 3,417,613 are probationers. The financial cost of supervising these people is staggering, but the cost to their families and victims cannot be measured. With three and a half million probationers already in the system and more coming every day, there is a clear need for good people to enter the profession. Although there has been some debate in the past about whether probation qualifies to be called a profession, it meets all of the following criteria for a profession:

- It is self-monitoring.
- It possesses a service ideal.
- Financial gain is not the primary motive.
- It is client-oriented.
- It requires specialized skills or training.
- It possesses a distinct terminology.
- There are professional organizations, artifacts, symbols, and journals.
- There is autonomy for members in decision making.

While there still may be some probation officers in the field without degrees who were "grandfathered" in, most possess at a minimum a bachelor's degree. As Table 1.2 shows, across the country, roughly 75 percent of the states require officers to have a degree and about 30 percent require a combination of education and related work experience. Standards emphasize that these degrees should be in some human service field or human relations type field such as criminal justice, social work, sociology, or psychology. Incoming officers increasingly are required to have experience working in the human service area or have an advanced degree such as a master's degree in social work or counseling. Most officers are required to complete a minimum number of training hours annually in areas applicable to their duties as Table 1.3 shows. In addition, a number of professional organizations welcome probation personnel and provide training, technical support, journals, and other literature to help officers meet the ever-expanding demands on their time and talents.

Table 1.2 Minimum Education Requirements for Probation/Parole Officers
As of February 1, 1998

State	ADULT Parole	ADULT Probation	JUVENILE Parole	JUVENILE Probation
AL	BA	BA	C	C
AK	BA	BA	1	HS
AZ	BA+Exp	C	BA	C
AR	BA or Ed/Exp	BA or Ed/Exp	C	C
CA	BA	C	BA	C
CO	BA	BA	BA or Exp	BA
CT	HS	BA+Exp	BA	BA+Exp
DE	BA+Merit Test	BA+Merit Test	BA+Merit Test	BA+Merit Test
DC	BA	BA+Exp	BA+Exp	BA+Exp
FL	BA	BA	BA+Exp	BA+Exp
GA	BA	BA	BA	HS
HI	BA+Exp	BA+Exp	BA+Exp	C
ID	Knowlg,Tr,Exp	C	—	C
IL	BA	C	BA	C
IN	BA	C	BA	C
IA	BA	BA	BA	BA
KS	BA	—	BA	—
KY	BA	BA	BA	BA
LA	BA	BA	BA	BA
ME	BA+Exp	BA+Exp	BA+Exp	BA+Exp
MD	BA	BA	BA or Exp	BA or Exp
MA	BA+Exp	C	BA+Exp	C
MI	BA	BA	BA	BA
MN	HS	HS	HS	HS
MS	BA+TEST	BA+TEST	BA/MA	BA/MA
MO	BA	BA	BA	BA
MT	BA	BA	BA+Exp	BA+Exp
NE	HS	BA	BA	BA
NV	BA	BA	BA	BA
NH	BA	BA	BA	BA
NJ	BA, Test, Tr Acad	BASoc Sci	BA, Test, Tr Acad	BA Soc Sci
NM	BA+Exp	BA+Exp	BA	BA
NY	BA+Exp	C	BA+Exp	C
NC	BA	BA	BA	BA
ND	BA+Exp	BA+Exp	BA+Exp	BA+Exp
OH	BA	BA	BA	C
OK	BA	BA	BA	BA
OR	BA	BA	BA	C
PA	—	HS	C	BA
RI	BA+Exp	BA+Exp	BA+Exp	BA+Exp
SC	BA	BA	BA+Exp	BA+Exp
SD	BA	BA	BA	BA
TN	BA	BA	BA	BA
TX	BA+Exp	BA+Exp	BA	BA
UT	HS+Exp	HS+Exp	HS	HS
VT	HS	HS	BA	BA
VA	BA	BA	BA	BA
WA	BA	BA	BA	C
WV	BA	BA	BA	BA
WI	BA	BA	—	C
WY	BA	BA	HS	HS

NOTES:
1 (AK) Juvenile parole is termed probation
C County/Local jurisdiction
— No response

Table 1.3 Mandated Training for Probation/Parole Officers
As of February 1, 1998

	NUMBER HOURS FIRST YEAR EMPLOYMENT				NUMBER HOURS AFTER FIRST YEAR EMPLOYMENT			
	ADULT		JUVENILE		ADULT		JUVENILE	
State	Parole	Probation	Parole	Probation	Parole	Probation	Parole	Probation
AL	480	480	C	C	12	12	C	C
AK	40	40	[1]	40	40	40	40	40
AZ	40	40	240	C	40	40		C
AR	148	48	C	C	40	20	C	C
CA	200	200	120	200	20	40	16	40
CO	40	40	40	40	40	40	40	40
CT	40	200	—	20	40	20	—	—
DE	270	270	80	80	40	40	40	40
DC	40	40	40	40	40	40	40	40
FL	360	360	80	80	40	40	40	40
GA	320	120	80	80	40	20	40	40
HI	16	16	80	C	16	16	40	—
ID	40	40	40	C	40	40	—	C
IL	40	C	40	C	40	C	40	C
IN	40	C	40	C	40	C	40	C
IA	80	80	80	120	40	40	15	15
KS	40	40	40	40	40	40	40	40
KY	40	40	128	128	40	40	40	40
LA	320	320	80	80	40	40	40	40
ME	100	40	40	100	40	40	40	40
MD	198	264	40	40	18	18	40	40
MA	40	40	80	40	40	—	—	
MI	40	40	40	40	40	40	20	20
MN	40	40	40	40	40	40	40	40
MS	400	400	40	32	40+	40+	40+	40+
MO	130	130	40	40	N	N	40	40
MT	40	40	40	40	40	40	40	40
NE	120	120	120	120	40	16	40	16
NV	40	40	40	40	40	40	24	24
NH	60	60	60	60	60	60	60	60
NJ	320	—	320	—	40	—	40	—
NM	64	64	120	120	40	40	40	40
NY	240	C	120	C	40	21	40	C
NC	160	160	36	36	40	40	10	10
ND	40	40	40	40	40	40	48	48
OH	120	120	80	C	40	40	40	C
OK	400	400	40	40	40	40	40	40
OR	240	240	40	C	40	40	Y	C
PA	160	40	C	C	40	40	C	C
RI	40	40	20	20	—	—	20	20
SC	365	365	—	—	40	40	—	—
SD	64	24	24	24	40	16	16	16
TN	40	—	120	120	40	40	40	40
TX	72	40	100	40	40	40	50	40
UT	40	40	120	120	40	40	40	40
VT	120	120	40	40	20	40	—	40
VA	120	120	40	40	20	20	40	40
WA	80	80	80	C	30	30	20	C
WV	40	40	40	40	40	40	24	24
WI	185	185	185	C	185	185	—	C
WY	56	56	60	—	24	24	—	—

KEY TO ABBREVIATIONS:
C   County/Local jurisdictions
—   No response
Y   Yes
[1] (AK) Juvenile Parole is termed Probation

Many officers are working for probation and parole agencies where they supervise both probationers and parolees. In 70 percent of the states, there are provisions allowing for probation officers to be armed according to local or departmental criteria. In jurisdictions where weapons are permitted, they are a mandatory requirement in 24 percent of them. Also, in some jurisdictions (especially where probation and parole are combined), probation officers serve their own warrants and make arrests.

In addition to being armed for self-protection, in some jurisdictions, probation officers also may be certified as peace officers. Peace officer status has varying degrees of authority and responsibility depending upon the policies of the particular jurisdiction. For instance, in the federal system, probation officers are peace officer certified, but may use U.S. Marshals to execute warrants and make arrests. When probation officers are also peace officers, their powers tend to be limited to the scope of their employment, giving them power of arrest over probationers, but not over the general public. Peace officer status is useful for officers supervising sex offenders where they may need the authority to seize a computer or other evidence immediately and to officers working with joint task force operations that are targeting gang and drug activity.

There is continued debate over whether probation officers should be or need to be armed. Richard Sluder (*Corrections Compendium*, 1995) conducted a survey of probation officers, which found that 59 percent of those surveyed supported the option to carry a firearm while working. Sluder found a "professional tolerance, if not personal acceptance, of firearms as a necessary tool . . . but that tolerance dissipated quickly when the option became a requirement." Criminal justice students should be aware of the weapons argument and (as always) seek careers in agencies whose policies are compatible with their own philosophy and preferences on this issue.

Table 1.4   Beginning Salaries for Probation/Parole Officers
As of February 1, 1998

State	ADULT		JUVENILE	
	Parole	Probation	Parole	Probation
AL	20–25	20–25	C	C
AK	35–40	35–40	+	35–40
AZ	25–30	C	25–30	C
AR	13–20	13–20	C	C
CA	45–50	C	35–40	C
CO	30–35	25–30	30–35	25–30
CT	30–35	35–40	30–35	40–45
DE	25–30	25–30	20–25	20–25
DC	30–35	25–30	—	25–30
FL	20–25	20–25	13–20	13–20
GA	20–25	20–25	20–25	20–25
HI	30–35	30–35	30–35	—
ID	25–30	20–25	—	—
IL	30–35	C	25–30	C
IN	20–25	C	20–25	C
IA	30–35	30–35	—	BA
KS	20–25	—	20–25	—
KY	13–20	13–20	13–20	13–20
LA	20–25	20–25	20–25	20–25
ME	25–30	25–30	25–30	25–30
MD	13–20	13–20	13–20	13–20
MA	35–40	C	30–35	C
MI	25–30	25–30	30–35	30–35
MN	25–30	25–30	25–30	25–30
MS	25–30	25–30	20–25	20–25
MO	20–25	20–25	25–30	20–25
MT	25–30	25–30	25–30	25–30
NE	20–25	20–25	20–25	20–25
NV	40–45	40–45	35–40	35–40
NH	25–30	25–30	25–30	25–30
NJ	20–25	20–25	25–30	20–25
NM	25–30	25–30	25–30	25–30
NY	35–40	C	25–30	C
NC	20–25	20–25	25–30	25–30
ND	20–25	20–25	25–30	25–30
OH	25–30	25–30	25–30	C
OK	20–25	20–25	13–20	13–20
OR	20–25	20–25	25–30	C
PA	25–30	25–30	C	C
RI	30–35	30–35	30–35	30–35
SC	20–25	20–25	20–25	20–25
SD	20–25	20–25	20–25	20–25
TN	20–25	20–25	20–25	20–25
TX	25–30	20–25	20–25	30–35
UT	20–25	20–25	20–25	25–30
VT	20–25	20–25	—	—
VA	25–30	25–30	25–30	25–30
WA	25–30	25–30	30–35	C
WV	13–20	13–20	13–20	13–20
WI	20–25	20–25	30–35	C
WY	20–25	20–25	20–25	20–25

NOTES:
1   (AK) Juvenile parole is termed probation
C   County/Local jurisdiction
—   No response

Caseload sizes vary, but an average caseload per officer during 1997 was 175 regular probationers, 34 on intensive supervision, 20 on electronic supervision, and 62 on special (sex offender) supervision. In California, the average probation caseload in 1997 was 900 with regular supervision ranging between 800 to 1,000 cases. By contrast, in Maine, caseloads range from 70 to 180, depending on the region in the state (Camp and Camp, 1998). Probation officers may be paid for overtime or work flex schedules, which include nights and weekends. Where overtime is paid, it may be in compensatory time rather than in monetary compensation. There are even some part-time officers where two officers work the same caseload. Officers working in rural jurisdictions, large cities, and with juvenile offenders may travel extensively to supervise or transport their clients. This travel frequently is done in the officer's personal vehicle.

Probation officer salaries range from the lowest entry salary of $13,000 for a Kentucky probation and parole officer, to Alaska's $83,000 career maximum. Table 1.4 demonstrates the salary range for beginning probation officers. Initially, parole officers earn slightly higher salaries, but over time, probation officers' salaries are slightly higher. In 1999, career averages for probation officers were around $35,000 annually.

SPECIALIZED CASELOADS

To expedite the supervision of offenders and protection of the community, a number of specialized caseloads have been developed. Officers working these caseloads become experts in a particular area or problem and manage offenders who present unique or multiple problems—more so than the average probationer. Among the specialized caseloads found across the country are the following:

- Juvenile officers must be familiar with child and adolescent development and be able to work with youth, families, and a variety of agencies including schools, child welfare, and mental health.
- Court officers function primarily in the courts, presenting cases for revocation and carrying out the court's instructions for disposition. Field officers send their cases to these officers to take to court and resume supervision if the probationer is continued on probation.
- Officers charged with writing presentence investigations (PSI) do so to assist the court in its sentencing decisions. This job requires extensive interviewing and good writing skills.
- Officers who provide Intensive Supervision Probation (ISP) to their probationers make weekly reports. They conduct frequent field visits, require urinalysis samples from their probationers, and make curfew checks. ISP officers may perform surveillance and spend much time in the field, often after hours.
- Sex offender officers supervise sex offenders and provide intensive supervision as well as monitor the offender's participation in sex-offender treatment programs. These officers often work with treatment professionals as well as victims. They need computer skills to monitor those probationers who may use the Internet for obtaining pornography or engaging in stalking.
- Specialized caseloads for monitoring those with mental health problems have been developed to serve the mentally retarded or mentally ill offender. These officers work closely with local mental health agencies to ensure that offenders are attending and taking advantage of mental health services.
- All officers must understand the dynamics of addiction, how various substances affect the individual, and work with treatment professionals in making referrals and offering treatment services. Officers who also are certified substance abuse counselors may run groups for their drug or alcohol dependent clients.
- Officers with caseloads of those convicted of domestic violence work with mental health professionals and family counselors to

provide counseling for both offenders and victims, and to ensure the safety of the victims.

- Officers who deal with gangs spend a great deal of time in the field monitoring their probationers. They may work closely with the police in identifying and controlling gang behavior in specific neighborhoods, and in developing alternative activities for gang youth.

- The Interstate Compact provides for the supervision of offenders who move from the original jurisdiction of their probation (transfer caseloads). These officers handle a large amount of paperwork and must be familiar with probation laws of other jurisdictions and be able to deal with many different people, philosophies, and procedures.

In addition to these specialized caseloads, probation officers also may serve as training officers and provide training services for their department. Some officers supervise community service, life skills, or employment programs.

COMPUTER CRIME

Computer crime, a relatively new specialty for probation, can be expected to grow in the coming decade. Already, agencies such as the Federal Bureau of Investigation, the Department of Justice, the Department of Energy, the Federal Trade Commission, the Customs Department, and many state and local agencies are setting up computer crime units to detect and supervise crime in cyberspace. Probation officers across the country can benefit from the public information now available online as increasing numbers of jurisdictions make their records available on the Internet. Just a few of the databases available include the following:

- Vital statistics

- Motor vehicle information
- Occupational licenses
- Criminal histories
- Property tax/mortgage information
- Voter registration
- Weapons permits
- Bankruptcy
- Utilities

In addition, California, Alaska, Florida, Indiana, Kansas, and Michigan have sex offender registration on line for public access. The implications for probation are enormous. Eventually, current crime information networks will be expanded and computerized into one nationwide or even worldwide system. Officers will be able to track absconders through computer records. Monitoring of sex offenders' computer files will become part of their supervision. Stopping computer crime will require more computer expertise from probation officers who must supervise individuals using the Internet to steal and commit fraud.

ACA Standards

In addition to meeting the definition of a profession, probation benefits from the American Correctional Association's *Standards for Adult Probation and Parole Field Services* and *Standards for Juvenile Probation and Aftercare*. These standards are presented as the minimum requirements for probation departments and were developed in cooperation with the Commission on Accreditation for Corrections. Every facet of probation work is addressed in these standards and they provide consistency and a high level of professionalism for all jurisdictions that have adopted them. Among the many areas covered are the following:

- Mission statements
- Written policy and procedure manuals
- Organizational charts describing lines of authority and accountability
- Collaborative agreements with other agencies and probation departments, including the Interstate Compact
- Communication among staff and probationers
- Audits
- Physical plants
- Fiscal policy
- Human resource issues, including training requirements
- Case file management
- Confidentiality
- Violation procedures
- Use of force and firearms policy
- Collection of court-ordered money

PARADIGM SHIFTS

Probation is indeed a profession, but it is one with an image problem and an identity crisis. In August 1999, the Manhattan Institute released a report: "Broken Windows Probation: The Next Step in Fighting Crime" (Arola and Lawrence, 1999). This report represents several years of work by probation professionals and academics on the need to change and restructure probation services. It comes on the heels of some spectacular failures.

One of those failures was Jeffrey Dahmer, who was on probation while he carried out the murders and cannibalization of numerous young men. His neighbors had complained about the smell coming from his apartment. After he was arrested, his probation officer was asked if he had ever smelled anything at Dahmer's residence, and he answered that he had never been there. Dahmer's neighborhood had been deemed too dangerous for probation personnel to visit—it had been redlined.

More recently in the news is the case of Buford Furrow. Furrow was on probation in Washington State and had been ordered to turn in all his guns. He failed to do so and, instead, murdered a postal worker and ambushed a Jewish daycare center in California. *The Los Angeles Times* reported that the probation officer had not made a home visit or checked on Furrow's surrender of weapons.

U.S. Department of Justice statistics indicate that only 51 percent of probationers comply with and complete any special conditions of their court orders, and less than half pay their fines (Basile, 1995). Probationers account for more than 20 percent of all new felony arrests. Such information shows that there is a need to reexamine the profession and adapt to the needs of modern American society. Probation officers and managers must take leadership roles in changing these trends by working with the judiciary, other agencies, and the public. The following discussion on victims, cognitive learning, and "what works" is a starting point for officers who want to make a difference.

VICTIMS AND THE BALANCED APPROACH

Probation traditionally has focused so heavily on the offender that victims were ignored by the criminal justice system. In a report by Richard Lasater on the Spokane Pilot Project in Victim Awareness (1995), the author states that many victims "suffer long after the offender is tried, convicted, sentenced, has served their (sic) sentence, and has been released back into the community." This idea of service to victims must be included in any new directions the profession takes.

In this vein, Vincent D. Basile (1995), Field Service Supervisor of Probation in Massachusetts, supports the balanced approach and restorative justice (BARJ) model. This model moves away from a retributive focus on the individual offender to one of protection of the public while reintegrating the offender into society. Under this model, the offender is held accountable to victims and communities, the public is protected, and the offender is reclaimed through "competency development." Competency development allows offenders to develop skills that will make them employable and assist them in becoming productive citizens. Working with the community, probation leaders develop relationships with employers, schools, and other agencies to meet offenders' needs. Community input is sought in policy planning and service delivery. The balanced approach and restorative justice model requires a vision statement addressing all probation customers (not just the offenders) and calls for measurable goals.

To implement such a model, probation must be able to set goals and objectives and measure not only their delivery, but their effectiveness. Most agencies have a mission statement and have goals to accomplish it. However, it is imperative that probation personnel be sure they are measuring the right things. Service delivery which does not effect change is wasted service. Probation officers and administrators must look at how to measure the effectiveness of services rendered to offenders. Dr. Edward Latessa (1999), who has researched "what works," stresses the importance of measuring program effectiveness in reducing re-arrest, incarceration, technical violations, and increasing program completions by high-risk offenders. He also recommends measuring the quality of services delivered through regular evaluations and use of this data to improve service delivery. He cautions that established programs not be omitted from a rigorous evaluation process.

Dr. Latessa is a strong advocate of cognitive programs, which provide clients with ways to "reframe" the process of habit change. Many others join him in support for cognitive programs. In a 1997 report for the National Institute of Corrections, Bush, Glick and Taymans state that individuals can control their thoughts, thereby controlling their feelings. This leads to control over their life. Brian Cox (1997) says, "what we do in our minds controls what we do in our lives." Probation must begin to provide offenders with skills to identify and control their criminal thinking.

The "Broken Windows" report (Arola and Lawrence, 1999) boldly related public dissatisfaction with the field of probation, citing failures in public safety, in enforcing orders, and in helping offenders. Among the reasons for this perceived failure are inadequate funding, understaffing, and lack of research. The report cites criminologist Joan Petersilia's figures that we spend $200 annually per probationer, while we spend $20,000 to $50,000 annually for each individual in prison. As a result of this study, the authors of the report propose some specific changes, which they believe will make probation a viable part of the criminal justice system, and truly responsive to the public. Among their recommendations are the following:

- Make public safety the first goal.
- Move officers and programs out into the community. Make geographic assignments for officers instead of just having them handle a certain number of people on a caseload.
- Develop and enhance community input in policymaking.
- Make a rational allotment of resources; spend time and money on those dangerous to the public or on high-risk offenders.
- Enforce court orders and abandon permissive practices.
- Evaluate programs and allocate resources to what works.

Many probation officers in the field agree with these ideas and are attempting to practice them, but the profession as a whole must make a commitment to this idea before any widespread changes can occur. Probation officers and probation administrators must take the lead in changing the direction of probation so that the shocking statistics on recidivism among probationers can be changed for the better.

The debate over probation's future will continue, and we can expect the focus to change from the offender to a broader concern for services and methods that will benefit not just the offender, but all of society. Although paradigm shifts will change the face of probation in many ways, we can expect certain elements to remain.

THE PROBATION PROCESS

Probation is not a right, but a privilege. Although the law may specify that probation is a sentencing option, once convicted of a crime, the offender may be incarcerated instead. To initiate the probation process, offenders must request consideration for probation. Offenders' attorneys may do this, or the probation department may assist offenders in filing an application for probation prior to sentencing. Once placed on probation, offenders are ordered to report to the probation department, usually immediately, to begin intake.

An intake probation officer or case aide will meet with incoming probationers and review their court orders, departmental rules, reporting schedules, and verify personal data. If the officer performing the intake will not actually supervise the offender, a permanent officer is assigned. During one of their first meetings, the probation officer will conduct an assessment to determine the offenders' risk level and any special needs they have. Following the assessment, the officer and offenders should negotiate a supervision plan to address special needs and give the offenders time-oriented goals for fulfilling their probation conditions.

During the risk assessment, the officer will have assigned a level of supervision for the offenders. This level will determine how frequently the officer sees the offenders. With the passage of time, probationers may perform well enough to have their supervision level reduced to a less restrictive one, or their level of supervision may be increased due to violations. Practices will vary, but probation officers should be sure to document decisions to increase or reduce supervision levels using the approved evaluation methods and criteria of the department.

When offenders violate their court orders, officers must report the violations. Depending on the seriousness of the violation and departmental procedures, those with a violation report may be referred for an administrative hearing, or to the court for a revocation hearing. Administrative hearings are conducted by probation personnel, usually a supervisor, and are held at the probation department. A summons is issued by the probation department, giving the offender notice of the violation and time to respond to it. An attorney may or may not be present. In departments administered by the courts, the hearing officer may make decisions regarding the probationer's supervision, which then are referred to the court for the judge's approval.

In departments administered through the executive branch of government, the hearing officer's decision may be conclusive. For the most serious violations, or in jurisdictions where administrative hearings are not performed, violations are reported to the court. This usually will require a formal report to the state's attorney alleging the probation violation. A subpoena then is issued requiring the offender to report to court on the specified date, and although the right to a jury trial does not apply, the probationer will be entitled to legal counsel. A revocation hearing is an adversarial proceeding held in a courtroom and the defendant may appeal the court's decision. Defendants also may appeal decisions in administrative hearings through the appeals process of the agency.

At a revocation hearing, several outcomes are possible. Probation may be revoked and the defendant sentenced to a period of incarceration. The allegations may be dismissed and probation continued as originally ordered; the probation may be modified; or the case may be held in abeyance and set for review at a later date. Modifications usually include more restrictive conditions, but could be used to remove conditions as well.

Most probationers do not end up in revocation hearings but continue to report until their case expires. There may be provisions to allow for early termination or early release from probation in certain cases. Procedures for this vary. In some jurisdictions, the probation officer may be allowed to petition for the probationers' early release, while in others, the probationers must file a motion and have a hearing for early termination of their probation.

Due to the length of felony sentences, probationers may have many officers during the course of supervision, and their levels of supervision may change several times. When taking over a case from another officer, the new officer should take time to read the file in its entirety and be sure that all conditions and deadlines have been met. At the end of the probation period, the officer should ensure that all documentation is completed and the file closed according to departmental procedure.

PROBATION OFFICER DUTIES: COP OR CASEWORKER?

In spite of the future changes anticipated for probation, many basic probation officers' duties always will remain, and some would be enhanced under the restorative justice model. Probation officers are responsible for supervision of the offender. This includes seeing that the court order is followed and that any violations are reported to the court. It also includes collecting court-ordered money, making appropriate referrals, and documenting everything. Probation officers' duties can be broken down into four broad categories: supervision, reports to the court, collection, and service delivery and brokering. We will examine each category.

SUPERVISION

Probation officers must supervise the offenders assigned to them. This includes holding regularly scheduled meetings with the offender at the probation department, at the offender's home, job, school, or other locations such as a jail or the hospital. Officers regularly verify basic information on their probationers such as their address, phone number, and employment. Some offenders will move and not notify the officer— unless asked. It is essential that the probation officer know where their probationers can be found.

Supervision includes monitoring compliance with court-ordered conditions. The probation officer must verify attendance at substance abuse groups, completion of community service, participation in education programs, and so forth. Officers conduct assessments of the probationer's risk and need levels and write supervision plans accordingly. They then must monitor the probationers' progress toward fulfilling their supervision goals. The probation officer also is responsible for maintaining the probation files, which entails documentation in chronological entries (chronos) of all contacts, as well as preparation and preservation of various evaluations and reports.

REPORTS TO THE COURT

The probation officer reports to the court on their probationers' progress or violations. Included in such reports is the presentence investigation (PSI), which is a specialized report prepared for the court's use at sentencing. These generally are submitted after conviction and prior to sentencing, but some jurisdictions require officers to write postsentence reports in the case of new circumstances, a new offense, or technical violations of the probation order. Probation officers also testify in court, usually at revocation hearings. When reporting to or testifying in court, the probation officers are fulfilling their role as officers or servants of the court. Information the officer provides may be harmful to the probationer for whom the officer also may have acted as an advocate. This particular function of the probation officer's duties is sometimes problematic for officers and offenders both, but the officer's first duty is to the court.

COLLECTION OF COURT-ORDERED MONEY

Among the least-liked duties of most probation officers is that of collection of court-ordered money. Probationers will owe supervision fees, court costs, fines, victim restitution, and other fees. Less than half will pay these. It is the officer's duty to monitor the probationer's payments and address any deficiencies as soon as they occur. Allowing a probationer to slide on payments is a disservice to everyone involved. Probation departments and courts are funded at least partly by the fees collected. This eases the burden on the taxpayers and puts it on the offender, where it belongs.

Nonpayment of victim restitution is a particularly telling factor in the offender's rehabilitation. Offenders, who are stating with their words that they have changed, but who do not pay their victims, are sending a loud and clear signal that they may not be rehabilitated after all. Probation officers constantly must remind offenders of their financial debts. This will entail counseling offenders regarding prioritization of their financial resources, assisting in the writing of budgets, educating the offender about disposition of their payments, and reporting delinquent probationers to the administration or the courts for sanctions.

SERVICE DELIVERY AND BROKERING

Providing delivery and brokering of services is a part of the probation job that many officers prefer above all others. It allows the probation officers to fulfill the helping role that attracted them to the profession in the first place, and it is essential if probationers are going to change their behavior. After assessing the probationer or reading assessments from outside agencies and other professionals, an officer may refer a client to substance abuse education or treatment, educational or vocational services, mental health programs, community service programs, sex-offender treatment, parenting groups, anger management, and battering and family violence counseling, among others. A few points need to be remembered here:

- Many offenders will not want help or cooperate with referrals. Authorities say that workers should expect rejection from some clients, especially alcoholics. Nevertheless, community and societal resources must be applied to offender needs and problems.
- Some referrals will be restrictive on the individual's freedom or privacy and require a court order.
- Many offenders have so many needs that they could be referred to multiple programs. Prioritize their needs and risks and limit referrals to two or three at a time.
- Factors such as money, work schedules, childcare, and transportation can have an impact on the offender's participation in special programs. Consider all circumstances before making referrals.
- Staff cases with other officers and a supervisor before referring a probationer to any program not already court ordered.
- Once a referral has been made and the probationer agrees or is court ordered, accept no excuses. If the officer does not monitor attendance and participation, the offender will assume that the service is not so important after all and quit going.

As the reader can see from reviewing the preceding list of the duties of the probation officer, some of them can be conflicting. These conflicts contribute to the officer's stress and sometimes fuel the debate about probation's identity crisis. Writing for ACA's *Field Officers Resource Guide* (1994), William Burrell says that the probation officer's role is to monitor offenders, assisting them to access services which will enable them to change their behavior, and enforce court orders. This illustrates the dual role of surveillance versus service. While conflicting roles certainly exist, Burrell says that officers can clarify any conflict by remembering that the bottom line is always the court order.

PROBATION'S FUTURE

Although philosophies and policies may change, there is a continuing need for probation and for probation officers. Current recommendations from the What Works and Reinventing Probation projects (*see comments by* Evans, 1999 and Arola and Lawrence, 1999) can make the profession more viable in the new millennium. Although many officers already attempt to do some of the things suggested, the profession as a whole will need to be committed to these ideas and be consistent in their implementation. Among the suggestions are the following:

- Move probation officers into the field.
- Change work schedules to include nights, weekends, and holidays.
- Increase the use of graduated sanctions prior to revocation.
- Concentrate on high-risk offenders.
- Make assignments by geographic area.
- Abandon permissive practices.
- Increase probation's involvement with other agencies.
- Measure program performance and use this as the basis for allotment of resources.

It is an exciting time to be a probation officer. Opportunity exists for officers to shape the future of probation and thereby improve it and the lives of the men and women who are serving probation sentences. Probation administrators are looking for the best qualified people to become probation officers. Pay and benefits continue to rise. As we examine our profession and improve it, the prestige associated with probation also will increase. It is a field where human potential is precious and encouraged.

Key Points to Remember

The reader should be able to discuss each of the following items:

- John Augustus was the father of probation.
- Probation's roots are in social work.
- Some of the probation officer's duties are performing supervision/casework, reporting, collecting court-ordered money, and serving as a service broker.
- Restorative justice moves away from the retributive focus.
- Probation officers should practice what works in reducing recidivism.
- Probation officers can have a role in reforming probation.

The Ethical Probation Officer

In this new millennium, issues of right and wrong surround us. Daily we are bombarded by stories of unethical behavior on the part of public officials and those entrusted with the public good. Scientific and medical discoveries have surpassed our ability to grasp the ethical implications involved in many procedures. The probation profession is not exempt. Officers who are the best writers, interrogators or case workers in the department are rendered useless if they are found to be unethical. It is a basic premise that to supervise offenders and help them toward successful change, the officers who do the supervising must uphold the highest standards of behavior. Since this principle is integral to the whole idea of corrections, we begin with a discussion of ethics and the probation officer.

Probation officers have ethical responsibilities above and beyond those of the ordinary citizen. The emphasis on ethical behavior cannot be restricted to an annual signing of the code of ethics. Concern about ethics cannot be reserved for those occasions when someone gets into trouble. Ethics should be the subject of an ongoing conversation among criminal justice professionals everywhere. Probation officers are public servants, paid for serving the courts and the public. However, many individuals envy the guaranteed salary, insurance, pension plans, vacation, and sick time that most officers enjoy. Yet, with these benefits comes an obligation. Probation officers take an oath at hiring to protect and defend the Constitution. All these things obligate probation officers to a higher code of behavior than the general public. Not only must officers follow a higher standard, but this must be done in often adverse circumstances and among criminals who know no such standard.

A fundamental concept of ethical behavior for probation officers should be to "Walk the Talk." In their book *144 Ways to Walk the Talk*, Eric Harvey and Alexander Lucia (1994) emphasize that people must earn the right to hold others to high standards by meeting those standards themselves. This is walking the talk. Probation officers must earn this right, as well.

In the Texas Criminal Justice Assistance Division training on the code of ethics, officers are taught that a good governing principle for the code is the golden rule: do onto others as you would have them do unto you. This is a good place to begin. Officers should practice treating others as they want to be treated. You may not be able to ever envision yourself in trouble with the law, but perhaps you can imagine this happening to a close friend or relative. How would you want that person treated? Probationers are important and precious to someone. They are daughters, sons, fathers, mothers, siblings, and best friends. In those roles, they have needs and expectations of how they want to be treated. Seeing things from the offender's point of view can remind the officer of how important the golden rule really is.

Although probation clients are criminals, they are also human beings. The Judeo-Christian heritage teaches that human beings make mistakes, but can and do change. A basic principle of our democracy is that all people are created equal under the law and are entitled to certain rights. Officers mistreating or not respecting their probationers are violating a sacred trust and obligation.

THERE'S A RIGHT WAY AND A WRONG WAY

One of the most often-quoted principles in management training is that of doing the right thing for the right reason. Officers are obligated by law and by oath to do certain things, which may be unpleasant for them, the offender, or both. On those occasions, officers should examine their conscience to be sure that they follow the law and act with pure motives, not self-serving ones. Officers cannot rejoice when an individual's probation is revoked. This is a failure for the probationer and for society. Although officers must be vigilant to detect and report violations, they should not look forward to this. Correction and confrontation should be carried out in the spirit of rehabilitation and duty. Justice Potter Stewart has said, "There is a big difference in what you have a right to do and what is right to do." This is a good guideline for probation officers.

The following three basic elements should be helpful in maintaining ethical equilibrium:

1. The officer's personal behavior must be honest and above board.
2. The officer is a servant to the court, the public, and the probationer.
3. Decisions must be both legal and ethical.

WHEN YOUR WORD IS YOUR BOND

As officers of the court, probation officers are expected to be and assumed to be honest. In a dispute with a probationer, the officer's word usually will carry more weight than the offender's. This has been true historically and makes sense. An officer's word should be more reliable than that of an offender who is automatically suspect.

With such an assumption comes an obligation to ensure that our speech and actions are honest. While most officers never would dream of lying under oath, there are varying levels of omission and innuendo.

Deliberately withholding information is dishonest. It is an ethical responsibility of the probation officer to keep the court fully informed when making reports and recommendations.

Officers are asked for their opinions, and it is appropriate to give an opinion when it is so identified. It is not appropriate, honest, or ethical to add supposition and innuendo to reports as though these were fact. Much damage can be done when officers project their own imaginations onto the offender. Whether deliberate or unconscious, things assumed by the officer can end up being reported as facts observed. Decisions then may be made based on supposition and half-truth. This can happen quite innocently if an officer is not scrupulous in checking and reporting only factual information and always identifying opinion as such. Facts can be proven by evidence in court. Once all the facts are given, the officer may add an assessment of what the facts mean and make recommendations, but the officer always must take care not to pass on opinion as fact.

Honesty is reflected in small ways throughout the day. "Fudging" on time sheets or padding mileage reports are two examples of dishonest behavior, which some may consider harmless and acceptable. Putting off an unpleasant phone call and then "forgetting" about it is dishonest. To be honest, one must practice honesty all the time—not just under oath.

Probation officers often are encouraged to be role models. Offenders tend to associate with other offenders and have extensive experience with dishonest people. Many of them think that everyone is a liar or thief, but that not everyone gets caught. These probationers think their officer is dishonest also. Others may not be sure, but they hope that their officer is dishonest because this helps justify their own bad behavior. Some offenders, however, hope that the officer is just what they claim to be. A significant factor in the rehabilitative process is a positive relationship between the offender and the officer. The probation officer may be the only positive role model in some offenders' lives, making the relationship even more crucial. Given these circumstances, it is paramount that the officer be honest and ethical.

CONFIDENTIALITY

Probation officers see and hear fascinating things in the course of their employment. Some of the things they see are funny; some are infuriating; and some are heartbreaking. Officers need to be able to vent by talking about some of the situations they encounter. In some departments, there are crisis intervention groups or employee assistance programs that can respond when an officer has been involved in a critical situation and provide them the opportunity to talk things out. Such groups are a good idea and should be encouraged, especially in life-and-death or other traumatic situations.

Although crisis intervention groups are useful, most stress release for officers occurs in more mundane ways. The officers take stress home to their family, the beauty shop, or the bar, and this is where the officer can get into trouble. While regaling friends or acquaintances with the outrageous behavior of probationer John Doe, an officer may reveal information that should have been left at work. A well-meaning officer asking for prayer for a rape victim inadvertently may tell too much and violate the victim's rights. Officers must take care with conversations about their cases by asking these questions first:

- Is it necessary to discuss this?
- Does this audience have a right or need to hear this information?
- Who else may overhear and repeat or misuse this information?
- What damage can be done to the probationer, the victim, the court, or the department by revealing this information?

Letting it all hang out after work, on the weekends, or any day at the bar can be counterproductive. Not only might you reveal things that should be kept confidential, but others see you as a representative of your department, and you may cause other people to lose confidence in corrections. On this issue of the image of corrections, *see* Freeman (2000).

Probation officers are human and need to talk about their work when they get home. As we discuss in the chapter on stress and burnout, this should not dominate an officer's life or conversation, but it is normal for people to discuss their work with those close to them. Probation work is different from other jobs, however, and officers simply cannot repeat some things without violating their oath and the confidentiality of clients and victims. Officers should leave as much at the office as possible. When possible, talking to supervisors or other trusted officers about problem cases allows you to vent and get advice. When discussing work at home, take care not to divulge information that could identify the offender, the victim, or other parties.

Abuse of Office

By virtue of their position as officers of the court, probation officers have access to information and to people that the ordinary citizen does not. Officers have power over their clients. Probation officers' recommendations generally are heard and followed by the courts. This is a serious responsibility for anyone. When dealing with unpleasant offenders, officers must monitor their own emotions and prejudices. It is wrong to harass or try to punish people just because the opportunity exists. Officers always must remember that they are working in a coercive system. Offenders are not on probation by choice, but due to court order and threat of incarceration. Any sanctions levied by the officer must meet the criteria of the department and be approved by the court. They must be aimed at helping the offender to reform or to protect the public, and cannot be solely for punitive value. Following proper procedures, treating all people equally, and monitoring their own behavior can protect officers from abusing their power.

LOYALTY

One of the elements of most ethics codes is a section on loyalty. According to the noted psychiatrist, Karl Menninger, loyalty is based on a common ideal that people fight for, regardless of minor differences. This is very appropriate for criminal justice personnel. Probation officers share a common ideal although they may disagree on methods. Depending on the philosophy of elected officials and judges, methods may change over time, but the shared ideals and goals are constant.

When officers find themselves in disagreement with their judges, administration, or other officers, they need to remember that they do share common goals. Crime is the enemy—the enemy is not the judge or the officer across the hall. If officers find they no longer can respect and obey their employer, the officers must then decide if they can work within the system to accomplish change and if not, they should look elsewhere for employment. Loyalty prohibits probation officers from publicly ridiculing their bosses or other officers. Such behavior weakens the professional and does not serve the offender, the victim, or the public. And, in the long run, such ridicule does not benefit the individual probation officer.

As mentioned previously, professional people must decide what they believe and ascertain if they are working in agencies where those beliefs are upheld. Some things can be changed. And the officers can work toward changing those things. Others cannot be changed. If officers find themselves at odds with their department's philosophy or procedures, and there is no forum for change, it may be better to leave rather than cause disruption or be disloyal. It is possible that other probation departments may be operated differently and the officer may discover a culture in which he or she feels more comfortable. Other methods are not always wrong; they just may be different. In many cases, there is room for more than one point of view and more than one approach. Sometimes, making changes in the way things always have been done requires the use of careful preparation and planning rather than a sledge hammer.

THE APPEARANCE OF WRONGDOING

Most training on ethical behavior includes a statement regarding the appearance of wrongdoing and conflict of interest. These are gray areas that require a lot of thought. Officers must know what their agency or department teaches regarding officer/offender relationships, business involvement with probationers, and conflicts of interest. In some departments, rules are very specific and well known to all. In others, these issues largely may be ignored or left rather vague. As professional people, officers must establish their own guidelines if the department does not. Let us look at some areas that can present ethical problems for the probation officer.

BOY, HAVE I GOT A DEAL FOR YOU!

At some time or another, every officer encounters a probationer who has a business deal to offer. Depending on the type of caseload, this may be a good price on fresh tomatoes or a major real estate deal. Big or small, the officer should not hesitate to say no.

Business transactions with probationers are forbidden in some jurisdictions, allowed in some, and ignored in others. Although many departments do not prohibit officers from doing business with offenders, the possibilities for misunderstanding, corruption, and scandal exist and should be avoided. The most honest deal can appear improper to other people and, therefore, bring notoriety to the entire department.

Also, some offenders are mentally unbalanced and may misunderstand the officer's intentions. Others possess such a criminal mentality that they may lie about the business agreement and present the officer in a negative light. No matter how enticing the "deal," probation officers should make it a practice not to do business with probationers. By establishing this as a firm standard, officers will not be likely to stumble into traps of rationalization when opportunities present themselves. A predetermined policy also helps prevent personal feelings from influencing a decision and allows the officer to treat all clients equally in this matter. Regardless of whether the department has an official policy, the responsible officer will decide that doing business with probationers is unacceptable. When approached by a probationer, the officer honestly can say, "I make it a practice not to do business with my probationers." This helps keep the officer/offender relationship on a professional basis and protects the officer from accusations of favoritism or misconduct.

Although most officers easily can see the danger in buying real estate or a car from a probationer, they may not be as sensitive to less significant situations. As is often the case, it is the small things that plague people the most. An officer may frequent a certain restaurant and find that one of his probationers always waits on him. Another officer may make an appointment for a haircut and, upon arrival, find that the hairdresser is one of his probationers. A client may show up at the office one day selling fresh produce. It is possible to get caught up in such small things without thinking about the consequences. Remember, small things pave the way for bigger things. Although officers may get caught by surprise once, they should not put themselves in the position of returning to a situation where they are doing business with their probationers. This way, the officer is honest and looks honest as well.

POLITICS

In some jurisdictions, probation officers campaign for candidates for the bench, district attorney's office, or sheriff, while in other jurisdictions this is prohibited. Although officers will want to exercise their rights as citizens and should be active in the community, public support for political candidates is not a luxury officers should permit themselves.

On a practical level, officers must consider the possibility that their candidate may lose. In many jurisdictions, officers are appointed by elected judges. In all jurisdictions, officers are dependent on the services of the sheriff or district attorney at some time. Officers supporting the losing candidate may find themselves in a strained relationship with the victor, and it is foolish to make unnecessary enemies.

Beyond the matter of supporting the wrong candidate is the broader issue of revealing one's politics to probationers. Just as politics is not considered polite party conversation, it is not good officer/offender conversation either. An officer's politics may suggest prejudices or beliefs that can interfere with the rehabilitative process. Politics can be divisive, and officers do not need any more divisive issues between them and their probationers than already exist.

Finally, there is the very serious matter of campaigning during office hours. Even in jurisdictions where this is allowed, officers should consider the ethics of getting paid while trying to get a candidate elected. Taxpayers may not appreciate knowing that their money went to a political campaign. Probation officers should supervise offenders, not practice politics at work.

Just Say NO!

Eventually in every officer's career, a probationer will ask them for a date or make some sort of romantic or sexual remark. This probably happens more often to female officers, but no one is exempt. Although the obvious response is no, some people miss the obvious and say yes. Friendships or dating relationships with probationers are ethical violations that fly in the face of common sense and decency.

The probationer making the advance may be extraordinarily handsome or beautiful. The probationer may be on a misdemeanor case about to expire in a few weeks. The officer may be lonely and overwhelmed by attraction for the offender. People can rationalize a lot. Officers in this situation must say "no" instead. Remember that when the offenders make their advance, they already know it is wrong, but they are hoping that the officers would violate their own rules.

Officers must be aware of the possibilities for disaster in a relationship with a probationer. If discovered, the officer probably will be fired. In some states, criminal sanctions will apply. The officer's reputation will be ruined in the professional community and with the general public if the relationship becomes public knowledge. There is always the possibility that the offender set the officer up to obtain information or favors. Even if this is not so, the officer never will be sure. Because so many offenders are involved with drugs and alcohol abuse, the officer may be exposed to illegal behavior or even implicated in criminal offenses. Probationers talk to each other and frequently discuss their officers. Probationers involved with their probation officer likely will tell other offenders. This compromises the officer's ability to supervise anyone. Even if the affair is never discovered, the officer will live in dread that it will be.

Sometimes officers are approached by probationers who are not their clients, but reporting to another officer. It is still wrong and a violation of ethical behavior to become involved with these people. Caseloads change. Officers are absent and other officers must cover their caseloads. It is conceivable that the officer could end up supervising the offender anyway. Family members of the probationer can present other problems. It is not uncommon for the spouse, parent, or another relative of an offender to approach the officer with a romantic proposal. These advances also must be refused.

The officer should not be coy or make excuses. Laughter or ignoring these behaviors will not work. Postponing the decision by saying something like "Maybe when you're off probation" is also unacceptable. As professionals, officers must take responsibility for themselves and the oath they took. Blaming someone else (my supervisor wouldn't like it) will not work. A brief statement such as "No, it would be wrong for me to date a probationer and I won't do that" is usually sufficient. If the probationers persist, tell them to stop or you will notify the court of their improper behavior. Document this in the file and advise your supervisor.

This is not to suggest that probation officers never can have relationships with former offenders. People do change and ex-offenders who have proven their rehabilitation may become friends or partners in life at some point. It is important to be sure that these relationships do not develop in the course of the officer's duties, or with active probationers. It is prudent for anyone becoming involved with a former offender to consider several things:

- How long has the person been off supervision?
- How well did the individual comply while on supervision? Was the person really successful, or did the case just expire?
- Is the individual employed and self-supporting now?
- Does the individual use drugs or alcohol?
- Does the individual express questionable attitudes about the law?
- Does the person lie?
- What is the individual's attitude toward authority in general?

Answers to these questions can reveal warning signals that the former offender may not be fully rehabilitated and could reoffend.

Officers who become entangled with probationers on a personal level need to assess their own lives and ask themselves how such a thing happened. Is there dysfunction at home? Is the officer lonely or in emotional trouble? Did the officer not see the situation developing in time to stop it? Most departments and agencies have employee assistance programs or insurance for counseling. The officer involved with a probationer or contemplating this should seek out professional help and an adequate personal support system. Failure to do so can result in humiliation and ruin. There must be some absolutes in life, and, in the probation officer's life, this is one.

I'M OKAY AND YOU'RE NOT
(DIVERSITY ISSUES AND THE PROBATION OFFICER)

It is human nature to be repulsed by some of the things encountered in corrections. It is also quite natural to reject some of the behaviors observed, but officers always must take care to differentiate between what is behavioral and what is cultural or based on class. This is often a difficult concept on which to accept and act. Because probation personnel tend to be white (71.4 percent of the 57,317 currently serving—*see* Figures 2.1 and 2.3 for a breakdown of the ethnicity and gender of probation officers), many officers have limited experience with or understanding of other groups or cultures but often find themselves dealing with people different from themselves. A large percentage of the probationers are minorities — *see* Figure 2.2. Nationwide, 30 percent are black, but in some states such as Louisiana and Maryland, the percentage of probationers who are black is above 50 percent (Camp and Camp, 1998). Similarly, the percentage of Hispanic probationers is almost 27 percent in Arizona, but nationwide it is about 10 percent (Camp and Camp, 1998).

It is important to learn about the groups who are on your caseload so you can begin to differentiate between cultural norms and legal deviance. Also, understanding the individual's culture will enable you to communicate more effectively. This results in a win-win situation.

Officers who bring prejudices about race, religion, gender, or other biases into their jobs do the profession, the probationers, and themselves a great disservice. Contrast Figures 2.1 with 2.2 and figures 2.3 with 2.4. (on the next page) Nowhere in society are the issues of cultural diversity and prejudice any more critical than in criminal justice. News stories depict graphic proof of abuse of minorities by police and

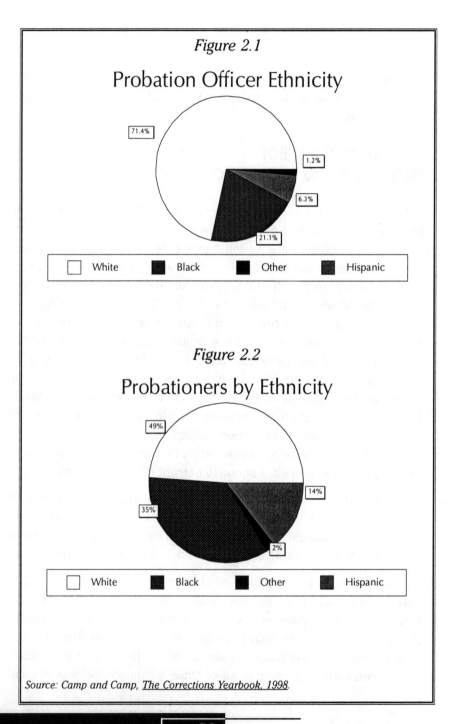

Figure 2.1

Probation Officer Ethnicity

71.4%
1.2%
6.3%
21.1%

White Black Other Hispanic

Figure 2.2

Probationers by Ethnicity

49%
14%
35%
2%

White Black Other Hispanic

Source: Camp and Camp, The Corrections Yearbook, 1998.

corrections personnel. Racial profiling is a hotly debated topic. Probation officers may not make arrests or guard prisoners, and, therefore, have little opportunity for corporal abuse, but the opportunity for prejudice and discrimination does exist.

At the turn of the century, the U.S. population is very diverse. Since the 1990 census, 30 percent of population growth has been from immigration, much of that from South America, other Spanish-speaking countries, and the third world. People of color have tended to assimilate more slowly than the white Anglo-Saxons of past immigrations, leaving them highly visible and vulnerable. Our diversity is so great that there are ongoing debates on who the minorities are, the politically correct names for various groups, and what to call the entire issue. Current terms are cultural diversity, multiculturalism, and cultural sensitivity.

Harold Lett, an intergroup relations consultant, names six characteristics that identify a minority group (Lum, 1996):

1. Ease of identification—members can be picked out in a crowd on sight or through casual contact
2. The slowness with which it is assimilated into the total population
3. The degree to which it exists in such numbers that it is an irritant by its presence
4. Its numbers and demands threaten the dominant group's notion of superior status
5. Intensity of the dominant group's reaction is measured by a history of emotional contact between them
6. The number and kinds of rumors that circulate about the minority group

The term minority can be misleading, since it may refer to a group smaller in number than the dominant group, or it may indicate a group less powerful than the dominant one. It is important to remember that

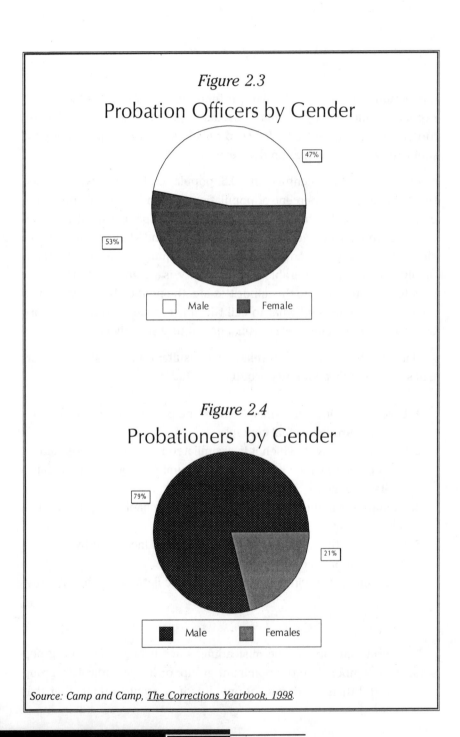

Figure 2.3

Probation Officers by Gender

47%

53%

☐ Male ■ Female

Figure 2.4

Probationers by Gender

79%

21%

■ Male ■ Females

Source: Camp and Camp, <u>The Corrections Yearbook, 1998</u>.

worldwide, whites are the numerical minority. In the United States, although white males are a definite minority in number, they continue to be the dominant power group. Minorities may display primary characteristics, which are visible and not chosen such as race, gender, or age. They also may display secondary characteristics, which may not be visible, but may be chosen and changeable such as political affiliation, religion, family status, or socio-economic status. Although probation officers will encounter all types of minorities, often the most problematic relationships will be due to racial, religious, gender, or sexual identification issues (*see* Figures 2.2 and 2.4 for a breakdown of the ethnicity and gender of probationers).

People respond to what they perceive and act on those perceptions, right or wrong. Our perceptions are based on our unique life experiences and the context in which they occur. It is human nature to seek out familiar and safe things. We are drawn to those people or ideas that support our own beliefs. Writing in *Police and the Community*, Louis Radelet (1986) says it is easier to think in stereotypes than in individualistic terms, resulting in what he calls "perceptual shorthand." Our perceptions become our opinions, which become convictions that determine our attitudes and actions. If our perceptions differ from those of our probationers, we can be ripe for prejudicial attitudes and behaviors.

Yet, prejudice always has existed. More than ninety years ago, W. E. B. DuBois, a writer with black and white roots, predicted that color would be the major issue of the century (Lum, 1996).

Although little has been written on this topic, the probation field also has been affected by prejudice. George Bridges (1999), a University of Washington sociology professor, has been studying issues of sentencing disparity. As part of that study, he examined presentencing reports on teenage boys in Washington State and found that based on the probation officers' reports, black youths received consistently harsher sentences than whites, even for the same offenses with similar circumstances.

Blacks were portrayed as disrespectful of authority, while whites were presented as victims of environment. Bridges believes the officers are not racists, but display "subtle and complex forms of prejudicial beliefs." The Washington study indicates probation officers can and do exercise prejudices, which adversely can affect casework and delivery of services.

Jacqueline Butler writes that the lack of knowledge and awareness about lifestyles and needs of various populations has resulted in poor service delivery to social work clients (Orlandi, 1995). Clearly, this can be extended to probationers as well.

What can probation officers do to combat the insidious effects of prejudice? First, probation officers (and people of good will everywhere) must acknowledge the value of diversity. Our differences can enrich us and make us stronger. These differences must be viewed in terms of behaviors and not as value judgments. Different means not alike, distinct, dissimilar, or unusual, but it does not mean better or worse. In an article for *Community Justice Concepts and Strategies* (Dunlap, 1998), Mark Carey lists some values which consistently have been found across cultural lines. Among them are honesty, integrity, fairness, compassion, respect, responsible citizenship, excellence, and accountability. Such research reaffirms what many human services employees already know—we are more alike than we are different. Regardless of cultural differences, certain basic needs and values always apply.

Probation officers can assess themselves to determine if they are acting prejudicially toward certain people or groups. Try this quick self-test. When discussing a case with another officer, how often do you identify your probationer by race, gender, or sexual preference? Do you identify all probationers this way, or only those who are different from you? When you use such identifiers, are they relevant to the case? For example: "I have this black guy on probation for auto theft, and he just won't report" or "I have this lesbian woman on my caseload who's not doing her community service." What is the significance of identifying these probationers by race or sexual preference? There may not be any significant reason. Officers who find themselves doing this repeatedly may have some prejudices they need to examine. Are you frequently accused of discrimination against a particular group? If so, consider the possible reasons. By practicing consistency in casework and following department policies, officers can avoid such behavior and protect themselves against false accusations as well.

Probation officers can learn about other cultures and groups. Knowledge is enriching and empowering. If it is true that we fear the unknown, then learning about other cultures can eliminate fear and free us to act in positive ways as human beings helping other human beings. Officers may take college or continuing education classes on cultural diversity. Workshops and seminars often are presented for professionals and encouraged by probation departments. Probation officers can seek out opportunities to interact with different kinds of people through travel or hobbies. These opportunities often exist already in the department as members of various minority groups take their places as officers and support staff. Reading literature and biographies of people from other cultures is very helpful in understanding them. Many popular novels and movies also break down the barriers of ignorance and prejudice.

The bottom line is that probation officers must actively develop and adapt their skills to deal with the diverse needs of their clients. Remember that many minorities have experienced racism, exploitation, oppression, and denial of their rights to various degrees. This experience may have an impact on how they respond to the authority of the probation officer. Knowing this, the officer is advised to attempt to overcome fear and resentment before proceeding with the helping process.

KEY POINTS TO REMEMBER

The reader should be able to discuss the following ideas:

- Officers must be honest in word and deed.
- The Golden Rule should be followed.
- Avoid the appearance of wrongdoing.
- Follow department/agency guidelines and training.
- Do not do business with probationers.
- Sexual or romantic relationships with probationers are always wrong.
- Diversity is good.
- Walk the talk.

Where Do I Begin?

CHAPTER THREE

So, now you are a probation officer. Someone gave you a badge and (if you were really lucky) a judge swore you in. You have an office (or at least a cubicle) in which to hang your diploma, and the business cards your mother ordered for you with the state seal. You feel very official and important. You also have a caseload of anywhere from 60 to 900 people (Camp and Camp, 1998), a phone ringing off the wall, probationers waiting to see you, someone in jail, court in an hour, and not a clue where to begin. We all think our problem should have priority, and some issues are quite serious. If you are to survive as an officer, you must get used to this. If you get organized, you also can maintain composure and direction throughout the day and take control over your job. Let us start with some basics.

The probation officer's job is an important one, but the fact of being an officer does not necessarily make the individual important. Learn to practice a little humility and do not be afraid to say "I don't know, but I'll find out." Never lose sight of the fact that as a probation officer, you are a public servant accountable to the community and taxpayers. This attitude should help you set some priorities, already. With your attitude on the correct course, the next step is to get organized.

YOUR OFFICE

Sometime during the first week on the job, try to get your office arranged for optimum productivity. Some people seem oblivious to their surroundings and can work anywhere, but others need a certain amount of order. Furniture placement is both an aesthetic and a safety issue. A neat, well-organized office imparts a feeling of confidence to your probationers. Other officers or your supervisor may need to work in your office on occasion and will appreciate your organizational skills when they look for files or forms. Begin with the biggest things first.

Your Desk. The desk is the biggest piece of furniture in the office, and it is a symbol of authority. Its placement may seem insignificant, but it is not. There are several things to be considered when placing the desk. For safety's sake, your desk should be positioned so that you can see people coming in and so that no one can block the door. Some offices are designed in such a way as to make this impossible, but follow this advice if you can. Most officers spend their entire careers without ever being in physical danger. On the other hand, you will supervise people who are angry, mentally unbalanced, or vengeful. Take no chances with your own welfare. If something as simple as desk placement can protect you, move your desk. Ideally, it should be placed so that the officer's back is not to the door and probationers cannot come between you, the officer, and the door.

Some officers like to arrange their desks and chairs to eliminate barriers between them and their probationers. This arrangement may be suitable for counselors, but it is not appropriate for probation officers. The barrier and authority symbolized by that desk are useful tools and may be protection in a crisis. Place one or two chairs opposite your desk and have your probationers sit in them.

Your Space. Some probationers will attempt to thumb through papers or rearrange objects on your desk. Offenders may be using this as a power play to gain control over the interview and put you off guard. Some probationers like to test a new officer to see how far they can go. By all means, let your probationers know that they are violating your space and you will not allow it. Most of this behavior can be stopped with a simple "What are you doing with the things on my desk?" If this is not sufficient, say something like "Please don't do that, Mr. Smith. I don't like for people to disturb the things on my desk." This almost always works, although you may need to repeat it on subsequent visits for the particularly resistant client.

Seating. Now about those pesky chairs—two are usually enough. Generally, adult officers do not want to encourage probationers to bring in their entire family. Even juvenile officers may need to limit the number of visitors accompanying their clients. The officers who know their probationers will be able to assess what friends or family members help the interview or impede it. Limit seating space and control who your probationers bring with them. Place the chairs opposite your desk and instruct your probationers to sit down. Do not allow them to stand over your desk or look over your shoulder. At best, probationers doing this are trying to gain control over the interview. At worst, they are agitated and placing themselves at a physical advantage for an attack. If individuals refuse to sit down or keep getting up, explain that you want to hear what they have to say, but you can only do that if they are seated. If a probationer still continues to stand, reschedule the appointment for the next day on the understanding that they will return ready to cooperate. Anytime you feel in danger, excuse yourself and go for help.

If you are working on a computer, some probationers will get up and walk around your desk to look at their files on the screen. Do not allow this. No probationer should be behind your desk or looking over your shoulder. Instruct them to be seated so that you can check your records. Say something like "Please be seated, Ms. Jones. I don't like someone looking over my shoulder while I am working." As with those clients who want to rearrange the officer's desk, these individuals usually will sit down when you ask them to do so. If not, stop the interview until they comply.

Some probationers will pull their chairs up very close to the desk and lean on it, invading your work space. This is sometimes another effort to intimidate the officer and take over the interview. In these cases, you may want to ask your probationers to move back so that they are not leaning on your desk. Almost always they will comply and not repeat this behavior again.

Equipment and Supplies. If your office design allows, have your file cabinet, computer terminal, trash can, and phone all within arm's reach. A rolling file cabinet with locks may be a good solution where space and office layout is problematic. Try to position large, heavy items such as hole punches and tape dispensers behind your desk and out of reach of the public.

When arranging your furniture and equipment, be sure you take into consideration your own comfort as well as security. Check to see if the lighting is adequate. If not, can your maintenance department give you more light, or do you need a desk lamp? Is your computer in an ergonomically correct position? Are the phone and electrical cords out of the way? Little things can add up to make your workday uncomfortable, if not dangerous. Plan ahead to eliminate unnecessary irritations.

Computers. Position your computer screen where your probationers cannot see it. You often will have information on the screen that is confidential and should not be available to offenders or the general public. If you do not think this is a problem, watch a computer terminal at any store or restaurant the next time you are out and see how easy it is to read while the clerks go unwittingly about their business. Employees at many businesses now clock in on the computer and beside their names one can find information such as their Social Security numbers and home addresses. Many offenders are computer literate and may be adept at reading and deciphering quickly what they see on your screen.

Desk Organization. Once you have the desk strategically placed, take a look at what is in it. If you are inheriting someone else's old office, the desk may be full of outdated memos or personal items. Pick a bottom drawer for your personal things and organize the others logically for the way you work. A deep hanging file is a good place for frequently used forms, blank stationery, memos, and a suspense file. The middle drawer or lap drawer is ideal for pens, pencils, and your time sheet. Use another drawer for office supplies and phone books.

Most departments and agencies have lists of frequently used numbers such as the district attorney, jail, and so forth. Put these in a folder in your lap drawer and do not post them for the public to see. Although some of these numbers are available to everyone, such lists often contain other information that the public does not need to know, such as officers' home addresses or birthdays. Keep these out of sight and lock them up at the end of the day.

Limit the clutter on top of your desk for the sake of your own sanity and for appearance. Too many photos or personal mementos can prevent an offender from finding a flat surface for signing a form. Too many files out on the desk at one time are confusing and can cause you to lose information or record it in the wrong file.

Develop a System for Incoming and Outgoing Mail. Most offices seem to come equipped with in and out boxes, which are rarely used for that purpose. Instead, they stack up with last year's memos and professional reading to be done. If you opt to use the boxes, be sure to use them properly. One of the principles of priority management is to use folders for pending work, reading, and projects. These are kept in a drawer and any time a document is placed in a folder, it is marked with a date to begin and that date is simultaneously recorded in the planner. This procedure forces you to finish your work that day, or schedule a date on which to do so. Finished work can be delivered to its destination on each trip to the mailroom and does not have to stack up on your desk.

Several years ago, a major company had an incoming/outgoing mail drawer procedure. Incoming mail was delivered daily to the upper left hand desk drawer, processed, and placed in the closed-out file or in the upper right hand drawer for forwarding to its next destination. The important thing is to have a system which works for you and that you will follow. It must make sense to you, be simple and quick to use, and be followed consistently. By doing so, you always will know where things are and they will not get lost in a "to do" pile.

Files. Be sure the file cabinet is located in an area that is convenient for access to your desk and anchored safely to the wall. On assuming a caseload, immediately begin to check the files to be sure you can account for all individuals on your caseload. Using your master caseload list, locate each folder and be sure it is filed correctly. If you find expired or closed files, pull these out to check for proper procedure. If any files are missing, immediately begin to locate these. If someone has borrowed a file (perhaps the PSI unit is using it to write a presentence investigation), make note of this on a sheet of paper and place this sheet where the missing file belongs. This helps you and anyone else who may be looking for the record. Files should be locked at the end of the day. Information in case files is often sensitive, and it is the officer's responsibility to secure these files.

Practice some safety recommendations from the Occupational Safety and Health Administration (OSHA) with regard to file cabinets. Although elementary to some, basic office safety is often ignored in offices everywhere. As previously stated, the file cabinet should be anchored to the wall if at all possible. Never pull out more than one drawer at a time. Position the heaviest loads in bottom drawers. Take care about storing heavy objects on top of the file cabinet. Do not leave drawers open, even for a minute; this is an excellent way to trip and fall in your own office.

THE CASELOAD

As soon as all files are accounted for, you should begin to read through each one. Although this may sound overwhelming, it is usually possible and always important. Scan the file for approaching deadlines or expiration dates, read the last few chronological entries for any problems you need to address now, and then read the entire file from beginning to end. Check to be sure that the court order and any amendments are in place and current. Take the conditions of probation and look for specific deadlines and special program assignments. If your reading indicates that a condition has been fulfilled, note that on the conditions. If a condition has not been met, make a note to review this with your probationer. When taking over a new caseload or starting a new job, you will want to make a list of any potential problems to discuss with your supervisor before you start seeing clients.

While reading the files, take note of addresses. If your probationer lives in a rural area with only a post office box or route number, be sure there are directions to the residence in the file. If not, make a note to get directions at your first meeting. A good officer knows where their clients live and how to get there.

TIME TO DECORATE

At the end of the first or second week on the job, it is appropriate to personalize your office. College diplomas and officer certifications are acceptable. Prints of favorite paintings or posters also may be acceptable if they are in good taste. Do not display items which may be controversial and alienate your probationers or other officers. Political statements and campaign literature are not appropriate. Anything which belittles or makes fun of one group of people should be avoided. When in doubt, the correct answer is usually "no." Do not bring keepsakes or expensive items to the office since the danger of damage or theft is high.

Proud parents and newlyweds like to bring pictures of their families to work, but officers should think twice before doing this. Some candid shots are not appropriate for the office. Furthermore, there may be sex offenders (including rapists and pedophiles) on your caseload whom you do not want viewing pictures of your family.

KEY POINTS TO REMEMBER

The reader should be able to discuss the following ideas:

- Humility; do not be afraid to say "I don't know."
- Get your office organized and then locate and secure files.
- Comfort and security are twin imperatives in the officer's office.
- Read every file, and make notes of problems to discuss with your supervisor.
- Note probationer's file of problems to discuss on the first visit.
- Be sure probationers' addresses are current and that you have directions to rural addresses.
- Office decorations should not be political, controversial, or too personal.

Casework, Court Work,
and Documentation

Many probation officers and others believe that the officer/ offender relationship plays a vital role in the offender's rehabilitation. A positive relationship is a "critical" factor in the offender's success or recidivism. Henningsen, Beto, Ross, and Bachrach (1999) confirm this belief based on a 1994 study of adult probation in Walker County, Texas, concerning probationer attitudes toward officers and probation services. Probationers reported that:

- Their officers explained rules and answered questions very satisfactorily (95 percent).
- Their officers had helped them succeed on probation (89 percent).
- They believed their officers wanted to help them with their probation (92.9 percent).
- Advice from probation officers was very helpful (95.7 percent).
- Their time on probation will help them stay out of trouble in the future (95.5 percent).

- Probation officers were responsive about seeing them in a timely manner (88.6 percent).
- The probation officers treated them fairly and with respect (96.2 and 94 percent).

Such information confirms the belief in the rehabilitative power of the helping relationship. In probation, this is complicated due to the dual role of helping and surveillance, but, clearly, it is workable. As part of the helping role, probation officers perform many casework functions. Among these are assessment of offender risk and need and referrals for services. Once these referrals are made, many offenders still will need assistance in accessing services. Mental ability, transportation, and financial status can be problems that will require further assistance from their officer before the offender can use services from other agencies. It is not enough to give someone the number to the local mental health clinic. A good caseworker will observe problems and help the offender overcome them.

Casework requires informed, current information on the issues that affect probationers' lives. Health, public welfare, and education issues are only a few that can have an impact on probationers who may rely on the probation officer for information and direction.

Some casework duties require listening and giving advice. Probationers who are struggling to get control of their lives may require reassurance that their new efforts are correct and will benefit them. When they make mistakes, they need to analyze what happened so they can make changes in their approach and try again. Good casework includes such elementary things as knowing the offender's neighborhood and the people with whom they live. Awareness of the client's employment situation and finances is good casework. Field visits are good casework. Being able to network with an offender's family members or other helping professionals in his or her life is good casework.

Advocacy for the offender, the victim, and the public is good probation casework. At the heart of good casework is a heart for people. Probation officers truly must care about other people and believe that people can change.

Court Work

Probation officers sometimes go to court. While some officers enjoy this exercise and look forward to it, others are anxious and often unprepared. One of the first things officers need to know is that the courtroom is rarely like those on television. Often, courts are noisy and disorderly. Attorneys may consult with clients in the back of the room while other cases are being heard at the front. Prisoners come in on rattling chains. Babies cry. People wander in and out incessantly, banging the door as they come and go. Intoxicated people come to court, and arguments can break out. Even if your court is quiet and dignified, it probably will not resemble the movies. Rarely can anyone beyond the jury box hear what is occurring. Many cases are settled in conferences that take place in the hallway or chambers and never actually come before the open court.

Officers should be prepared ahead of time for the atmosphere of their court and the philosophy of their judge. Regardless of how relaxed or how formal your court is, cultivate some basic habits. Dress for court. Most jurisdictions expect male officers to appear in a coat and tie and females to have on dresses or pant suits with appropriate shoes and stockings. This should be covered in new employee orientation or the personnel handbook. If it is not, ask your supervisor right away. Officers are called to court unexpectedly and need to be suitably dressed. There are judges who will not admit women in slacks or a man without a coat or tie. Know your judge and the judge's rules.

Female officers always should avoid short, tight skirts or tight pants. See-through fabrics are unacceptable as are stiletto heels. Jangling jewelry is distracting and may irritate the judge or a jury. Gum and sunglasses are also unacceptable, and men always should remove their hats when entering the courtroom.

Be on time! In fact, it is a good practice to go early. Some judges will begin proceedings whenever they get to work, regardless of the time set on the docket. Arriving late can be disruptive and can annoy the judge. Officers arriving too late may find that the hearing was held without them. Go early and wait your turn.

Demeanor and body language are important in court. You have a right to be there, and you have something important to add. If your court does not have designated seating for officers, find a seat close to the front and sit down. Sit up straight, look alert, and do not talk with other people in the courtroom once proceedings begin. Quietly review your notes and listen until you are called or dismissed. Once in the courtroom, try to stay put and not join the seemingly endless procession in and out of the door. An exception to this is the case when the defense asks the court to "invoke the rule." If this occurs, all witnesses expected to testify will be asked to wait outside the courtroom until called. After testimony, these same witnesses usually will have to leave the courtroom until the proceeding is concluded.

Before you testify, you should have been contacted by the state's attorney or prosecutor. If this did not happen, try to set up a meeting or telephone conference ahead of time. Many overworked prosecutors do not know until the day before court which cases they are trying and will appreciate an update from the officer. Find out how they like to question, and ask what they know about how the defense does a cross-examination. Review the file for pertinent facts, and write these down in chronological order on a small pad, which you will take to the witness stand. Unless the court demands, do not take the file onto the stand. Once you carry a file to the witness stand, the defense may decide to read it in its entirety, using this to distract you and confuse issues. Know your case.

Looking at notes is fine, but do not be totally dependent on them. This hurts your credibility and the case.

Watch other witnesses to see how the swearing in takes place. If you are the first witness and do not know the courtroom, follow the lead of the bailiff. Speak loudly and clearly and wait until instructed to be seated. Be sure that you are comfortable in the chair and adjust the microphone if there is one. The prosecutor will question you first. Listen carefully to the questions and wait a second before answering. This way you can formulate your response and be sure that the prosecutor has finished talking before you start speaking. If you do not hear a question or do not understand it, say so and ask that it be repeated.

It is okay to say "I don't know." You may be asked questions that you have no way of knowing or for which you just were not prepared. If the question is about a matter that you should know or can find out, say "I do not have that information, but I can get it for you." Do not qualify your answers with phrases such as "I guess" or "I think." State only the facts you know, and you will not need to guess. When asked your opinion, give it concisely. For example, you might say "It is my opinion that the probation department has exhausted all options available for this individual and that incarceration is the only option left." Avoid use of the words "always," "never," and the phrase "to tell the truth." If you testify that your probationer "always" or "never" does a certain thing, his or her attorney probably will find at least one exception to disprove your statement. Use of the phrase "to tell the truth" indicates that sometimes you do not tell the truth, but today you are. Do not open yourself up to attack from the defense this way.

If you make a mistake during testimony, say so. Something like, "Please let me correct the figure I gave earlier. The record indicates the defendant has paid $1,200.00, not $900.00, as I stated previously." Generally, you do not want to volunteer and answer questions not asked. However, when being questioned by the prosecutor, if you see they are missing a pertinent fact, you may want to try and get that on the record. The defense may object, but it is worth a try. As you become accustomed to your prosecutor and judge, you will know how much latitude you have on the stand.

Some experts say that you should look at the judge when answering questions from the attorneys. This may or may not be appropriate. Some courtrooms are arranged in such a way as to make this impossible or awkward. Some judges do not look at the witnesses. Try to get a feel for this before you go on the stand. It is more natural to look at the questioner. Some judges like to question witnesses themselves, and you certainly will look at the judge when the judge speaks to you. If you should end up in front of a jury, look at them when responding to questions.

Once the prosecutor has finished, the defense will question you. This can be easy or difficult, but it is not personal. Some defense lawyers like to take a very adversarial approach with the state's witnesses. Expect this and do not let it distract you. As with the prosecution, listen to the questions and pause before answering to be sure the defense has finished speaking. Organize your answer in your mind. Feel free to ask the defense to repeat anything you did not understand or hear. Do not volunteer information; answer only what the defense asks.

In most courts, the probation officer will be asked to identify the defendant. Do not point to your probationer unless instructed to point. Identify the probationer with a statement such as "That's Mr. Brown at the defense table next to attorney Smith." You probably also will be asked how to you came to know the defendant. Your answer will be that this person is on probation and state how long you have supervised him or her. It is possible that you may be asked to identify an absconder who never reported to you, or another officer's probationer. If you find yourself in this situation, there are several possibilities. If there is a picture in the file, you may be able to identify the individual from it. If you visited the probationer in jail when he or she was arrested, you can identify the person based on that visit. If you have neither of these options, try to introduce yourself to the offender at court and verify that you have the correct defendant.

After the defense cross examines you, there will be an opportunity for the prosecutor to clear up anything brought out by the defense, and then the defense has one last turn at questioning you. Wait until the judge excuses you before you leave the witness stand. Return to your seat and wait for the conclusion of the hearing. The judge may ask you for additional information or give you instructions after you leave the stand. Be prepared for this, and document the outcome of the hearing in your file. If there is a continuance, be sure to note this on your calendar when you return to the office.

The probation officer's role in court proceedings is to present information clearly, concisely, and accurately so that the judge can make a decision regarding the defendant. If your opinion is solicited, be prepared to offer it in a professional, thoughtful, and objective manner. This is a person's life and that person is precious to someone. What we do with our probationers affects many other people.

The Written Word

Closely related to courtroom work is documentation. Many officers think paperwork is a dirty word and hate report writing; however, good documentation can save a case and protect an officer. One of the most quoted statements in probation is "If it isn't written down, it didn't happen." Document office visits and phone calls immediately. Document field visits as soon as you return to the office. Keep copies of correspondence, especially violation letters mailed to probationers. If mail is returned to you, keep it in the file to prove that you mailed it to the address supplied by the probationer. Document facts so that anyone picking up a file in your absence can understand what is going on and take over supervision.

If you are required to write an assessment of your opinion, be sure that it is as objective as possible. Remember that "chrono" entries can be introduced as evidence in court. Caustic or sarcastic remarks are out of place in chronos and can come back to haunt you. Keep an orderly flow to chronos. What facts were developed? What agreement or plan did you make with the probationer? What is your assessment of the situation? Be sure your writing is legible and your prose is intelligible and coherent.

When writing a presentence report for court, find out what form your jurisdiction uses. Some departments use preprinted, fill-in-the-blank forms for presentences; others require a full narrative version. Some judges do not read past the first page. Others want everything you know about the case. Ask your supervisor and have the supervisor or an experienced officer read your report before you go to court. Even with spell check and grammar checks on your computer, errors will occur. Court is no place to look careless. Check everything and have someone else check also.

The presentence investigation (PSI) is an important tool, useful to the court for sentencing, the probation department for supervising, and the institutional division for assignment or parole decisions. A presentence investigation will require that the officer review the offense, the defendant's criminal history, employment, education, family relationships, mental health issues, or substance abuse issues. The officer will interview not only the defendant, but victims, the defendant's family and friends, and other interested parties. To ensure quality reports, follow some guidelines:

- Ask open-ended questions.
- Practice reflective listening.
- Make no judgments.
- Explain the sentencing process.
- Make no promises.

- Review the report to ensure objectivity.
The Field Officer's Resource Guide (1994).

Do not speculate about a defendant's attitude or value system. This only can lead to trouble in court when the defense attorney cross-examines you. Actions speak louder than words, and your interpretation of events could be wrong. Avoid saying that someone has a bad attitude, is lazy, or has poor morals. These are subjective terms and can indicate bias or prejudice on your part. Presenting facts will make your point. For instance, you have a healthy, thirty-year-old man who has not worked for two years. You have asked if he has medical problems, and he stated that he does not. He is not mentally handicapped. Even so, he does not work and lives at home with his mother who pays the bills, but will not give him money to pay his probation fees. Now, he has a new offense. There is no need to call this man lazy. The facts speak for themselves.

At the end of a court report, you usually will make a recommendation to the judge. Before you decide on your recommendation, you should review the continuum of sanctions in your agency or department and see what the appropriate step is on the continuum. Go over this with your supervisor. Some departments have review procedures or do administrative hearings before sending cases to court for revocation. Two heads are almost always better than one. Be sure you do this before you request revocation. It is possible to become too involved in a case and lose objectivity. The mission is not to lock people up, but to help them rehabilitate. If this can be done safely without incarceration, we must consider other options first. Do not include opinions unless specifically instructed to do so. Opinions do not outweigh facts. If a progressive sanction system has been followed and did not accomplish change, the consequences are probably revocation, regardless of your opinion. Opinion, even if qualified as professional, can become personal and this is dangerous ground for officers and offenders alike.

When you finish your report, review it for clarity: who, what, when, where, why, and how. Review it for spelling, grammar, and punctuation. Ask yourself if a stranger who knows nothing about the case would understand the information. Watch for abbreviations and jargon. Most judges will know what you are talking about, but this is unprofessional and gives the defense an opportunity for distraction. Be sure all facts are correct. Make an extra copy. If you must submit this report to a supervisor or judge by a certain date, be sure to do it early. If you send it through the mail or interoffice mail, follow up with a phone call or e-mail to be sure it arrived.

In all documentation, remember that it may be around for the life of the defendant's probation and beyond. Some reports follow the defendant into the prison system. You do not want to reread your own work in five years and find it lacking. As keeper of the probationer's record, you are establishing an official file, which may be used for years. Make sure it is good quality and durable.

KEY POINTS TO REMEMBER

The reader should be able to discuss each of the following items:

• Dual roles influence casework.
• It is a necessity to prepare ahead of time for court.
• Be on time, appropriately dressed, and have documentation.
• Listen to questions and ask for a repeat, if needed.
• State only what you know to be factual.
• Do not take your file onto the witness stand.
• Document everything.
• Make your notes, chronos, and reports legible and coherent.
• Remember, this is someone's life, you may make the difference.

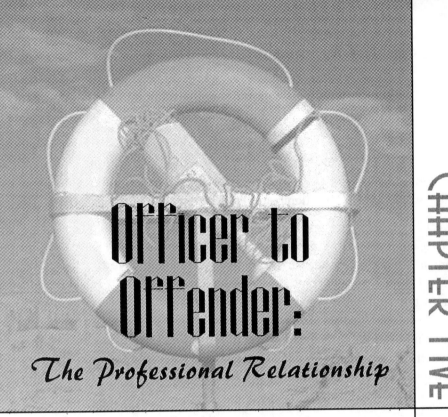

Officer to Offender:
The Professional Relationship

What should the relationship be between a probationer and a probation officer? This question often is asked during hiring interviews for new officers. You always can expect to hear "fair but firm." In addition to that response, there are a myriad of other ideas and theories of how officers should relate to their clients. Most officers will exhibit characteristics of more than one style of supervision.

At the beginning of your career, take some time to reflect on what your philosophy is and what your approach will be. Study the policy and philosophy of your department. What written and unwritten rules are already in place governing the officer/offender relationship? What does your supervisor or chief believe? Whose casework do you admire? And, finally, ask yourself which approach or style is most comfortable for you. The kind of authority that officers have is not natural and requires serious thought. You are having an impact on human lives and need to find a style that serves the courts, the public, the clients, and your own sense of order and decency. Usually one style will dominate an officer's work, although any officer may display various styles or play different roles, as the need arises. The following synopsis of common probation officer styles is deliberately exaggerated for ease of identification. After you read it, consider which style dominates your behavior.

Investigator. The investigator is the officer who really wanted to be a detective, but for whatever reasons, did not join the police force. These officers are most interested in the actual search and investigation process. They are usually good at following paper trails, and they also will know the neighborhoods and hangouts their probationers frequent. On field visits, they are able to obtain information just by observing the house or neighborhood. They know which probationers associate with each other and who has gang affiliations. If these officers are also good at documentation, they are powerful witnesses in court.

Investigators may not be particularly interested in the rehabilitative process or develop the kind of rapport with their probationers that makes them a role model. These officers are puzzle solvers. They can provide the who, what, when, where, how, and sometimes why, but they may not be strong change agents. The investigator has invaluable skills that can benefit an entire unit or department. All probation officers should have some of the investigator's characteristics, but there's more to the job than sleuthing.

Interrogator. The interrogator often is related to the investigator, but they are not the same person. The interrogator is an excellent interviewer. These officers can get information from a rock. An office visit with one of these officers will result in extensive family histories, criminal histories, and descriptions of crimes or other illegal behaviors. They are like bulldogs in their persistence and single-mindedness.

The interrogator is interested in getting truth. They understand that most probationers lie to their officer at least part of the time, and they do not accept any lies. They are always on a mission to get the real facts. They are not concerned about how the probationer feels and do not worry that someone will think they are being labeled a liar. They just want the facts. Interrogators are useful in getting complete and accurate information. Like the investigator, every unit or department needs at least one of these. All good officers should have some interrogation skills; however, having all the truth and nothing but the truth is still no guarantee of success in the rehabilitative process.

Police Officer. The police officer is often a frustrated cop at heart. These folks are very focused on the letter of the law, and they are looking for violations. Like a traffic cop staked out at the city limits sign, these officers are looking to catch their probationers doing something wrong. With offenders, this is not very difficult. Because a major function of the probation officer's job is to protect the public and enforce the conditions of probation, the police officer's mind-set is useful. All officers need to remember these duties and take them seriously, but we must not lose sight of the human element of the job. It is possible to look so long at bad behavior that human needs are obscured. Police officer-type officers have to remember to use the information they gain to demand change from their clients.

Executioner. The executioner is similar to the police officer, but these officers are not satisfied with catching wrongdoing. They want to impose maximum punishment. They believe everyone should be revoked for any violation. They do not support good time or parole, and they may approve of increased use of the death penalty. The executioner knows that there are natural consequences for behavior and holds people accountable for their actions.

We all can take a lesson from the executioners. Sometimes officers do not report violations as they should because they already have decided on what the sanctions should be. These may be lesser sanctions than what the court would have assessed. The executioner never would usurp the court's authority in such a way. The ideal is an officer who does not hesitate to notify the court of violations, but who also can make objective recommendations regarding sanctions. Many people are incarcerated who do not need to be. Catching someone is not enough; we must have positive alternatives to offer if they are to change their behavior.

Social Worker. The social worker is a term sometimes used in jest by probation officers, and many do not want to be accused of doing social work. There is a perception by some that social workers are too soft on offenders and may be easily deceived or that they do not hold probationers accountable for their actions. The reality is that probation is a form of social work, and all officers can benefit from social work theory. Social workers are very concerned with the internal, societal, and familial causes of crime. They tend to be concerned with probationers' feelings and needs. These officers often establish excellent rapport with their probationers and often are able to get them to participate in rehabilitative programming. Their allegiance may be more to the individual probationer than to the court, which can be problematic if the officer is distracted from the overall probation mission. Not only are officers responsible for rehabilitation, but they also are responsible for the protection of the community. Social workers may have trouble with this, but the probation officer's ultimate allegiance is to the court.

All officers can benefit from watching the social worker. They often represent the ideal in behavior. They are compassionate and constant reminders that probation is a human service and probationers must be treated as human beings. The social worker knows that people are flawed creatures with the potential to change, and they are very dedicated to helping others. The best probation officers know that people are flawed and with potential to change, but that everyone will not change. They also know that it is the probationer's responsibility to change, and it is the officer's responsibility to supervise the probationer's efforts, report these to the court, and protect the rest of society.

Ideally, the probation officer should combine characteristics of all these types. The officer must reach a point of being comfortable with their authority. As officers mature in experience, they usually learn to emphasize different aspects of their role, according to the situation or needs of the probationer. Regardless of variables, there is one constant that must prevail in officer/offender relationships. That constant is professionalism.

WHAT IS IN A NAME?

The term professional has been used to the point of overkill. Everyone likes to be called a professional. As stated earlier, there is an ongoing debate about probation as a profession. Nevertheless, due to the education, specialized training, and the great latitude permitted officers in decision making, probation officers certainly qualify as professionals. As such, there are some specific behaviors that can enhance and maintain professionalism. Let us start with the problem of familiarity.

We all know the old saw—familiarity breeds contempt. There is a lot of truth in this as it applies to corrections. Probation officers cannot be friends with their probationers. Start with how you will be addressed. Many departments will not allow probationers to address their officers by their first name. If your department has such a rule, by all means, follow it. If there is no such rule in your department, consider making it one of your own.

Your probationers should address you with a title (Mr./Mrs./Ms.) and your last name. If your last name is particularly difficult and you have a probationer whose mental or speech abilities are limited, it is acceptable to allow them to call you by your title and first name. Be sure there is a genuine need to loosen or lower standards. There are many probationers who will try to co-opt the officer by just such small things as a name or title.

Probation officers should extend the same courtesy to their probationers that they require from them. Address adults by their title and last name. When working with juvenile offenders, it generally is acceptable to call them by their first names. The difficulty with juveniles is usually parents who want to be too friendly with the officer. Do not allow this behavior any more than you would allow it from a probationer. The families of your probationers are also your clients. Frequently, they are offenders also, even if they are not on probation. They probably bear some responsibility for the probationer's criminal behavior and may be in need of services themselves. Family members also are adept at co-opting officers by being too familiar. Keep them on a last name basis just as you do your probationers.

At your first meeting with the probationer, introduce yourself with your first and last name. Say "I like for my probationers to call me Mr. Jones, and I'll call you Mr. Smith. Is that okay?" Most people will agree and try to comply. A few will challenge you or question this. Explain that yours is a professional relationship, and it is your policy (or the department policy) that first names are not used. Any time probationers slip and call you by your first name, correct them. Once you have stated your position, if the offender continues to use your given name, consider this a power play designed to distract you or detract from your authority.

Some officers believe that the use of first names expedites the rehabilitative process. Sometimes they may be right, but in criminal justice, it is more likely that the offenders or their families are attempting to manipulate the officer by use of first names. This is a small thing that paves the way for other things, which ultimately erode your authority and your perspective.

The seemingly small barrier of formal address can help you maintain your temper and composure when being verbally attacked. It is just harder to insult someone when you use a formal name. This practice also can help protect you from accusations of mistreatment or discrimination. If everyone you see is "Mr. Smith" or "Ms. Jones," you are less likely to be accused of treating one group of people better or worse than another. The use of a formal address sends a message to your probationers that you are taking care of job duties and are not open to personal relationships.

WHOSE BUSINESS ARE WE DISCUSSING HERE ANYWAY?

Probation officers never should discuss their own personal business with a probationer. Whether it is your address, your politics, or where you like to eat, this is inappropriate conversation between officers and offenders. Probationers are not your friends. They do not come to "visit" with you because they like or admire you. Probationers are criminals. They have broken the law and are under a jail or prison sentence. They come to see you for a specific purpose, and their probation should be the subject of your talk.

A pleasant greeting of "Is it hot enough for you?" is fine, but do not waste the probationer's time or the state's money in any long discussions about issues not relevant to their probation. Texas adult probation officers follow a system for office contacts which, when used correctly, keeps the officer on track and serves as a reminder to check on any pending problems. This PDAP system is good because each visit has a **p**urpose or problem. The information or **d**ata gathered should pertain to the pending problem, lead to an **a**ssessment of the situation and a **p**lan agreed upon by officer and offender. If an officer is doing all this, there is not much time for small talk.

A probation officer should not be giving out personal information. Do not offer your address to your probationers. Although the person you give this to may be trustworthy, they probably know lots of people who are not. Sooner or later, they will tell someone not so harmless where you live. Probationers already know when you are not home. Office hours are obvious. If you decorated your office with pictures of your family, they know who lives with you, so they know when your spouse or children are home alone. They probably know your car on sight and may have speculated about what other valuables you own based on your taste in cars, clothes, and jewelry.

Even joking about how poorly probation officers are paid can encourage certain offenders to think they can bribe you. Never reveal your financial status to an offender, and talk about your drinking habits or sex life is out of the question. Information about where your children go to school or where your spouse works should not be given out to your probationers.

Anything that would allow a probationer to know your routine should be avoided. If you have a probationer who knows you golf because they saw a golf umbrella in your office, they may ask where you play. A probationer seeing you at a restaurant on Friday night may ask if you eat there often. These kinds of questions may be harmless ways of breaking the ice, but they also can be ways for the probationer to get information about you. At the least, this can be awkward. At the worst, it could be dangerous. Downplay all such inquiries and do not give out information. If probationers persist, remind them you are there to discuss their probation, not your life. This usually will quiet the noisiest client, but if not, document and report this to your supervisor.

But He's My Neighbor!

What happens when a probationer turns up in your office and you discover that they live three doors down from you or attend the same civic club or belong to the same parent/teacher organization? These things do happen. See what your department's policy is and follow it. If there is no clear cut policy, consider these guidelines.

Probationers discovering their officer is also a neighbor or other club member probably will be nervous and embarrassed about the connection and want to ignore it. In this case, explain that you have notified your supervisor and it is your practice not to discuss probation business outside the office. You can agree to avoid each other except for your probation duties and assure them that as long as they comply with their probation order, you have no reason to interfere with their lives.

Problems develop when your probationer is someone you have a relationship with in the neighborhood, community, or family. If this occurs, notify your supervisor immediately. It may be impossible for you to supervise these people due to your shared history, and you will need to request such individuals be transferred to another officer. Some officers work in small towns where it is a given that everyone knows each other, and there is no one else to supervise the offender. If you are in such a situation, talk to your supervisor, chief, or judge and document this in the file. This will help protect you against allegations of impropriety later. You will need to practice constant vigilance to avoid being drawn into questionable circumstances.

Just Say No!

As discussed previously, romantic or sexual relationships with probationers are always out of bounds. This is covered in more detail in the chapter on ethics, but it bears repeating that such relationships are inappropriate, unethical, and sometimes criminal. If approached by a probationer with a romantic or sexual proposal, just say no.

No Games

In *Games Criminals Play* (1981), there is a self-test for corrections officers to see how susceptible they are to manipulation. The characteristics they list as risky include the following:

- Being overly friendly with most people
- Being so sympathetic to others' problems that rules seem secondary

- Being timid
- Being trusting
- Being unable to handle compliments in a businesslike manner
- Being desirous of helping the underdog
- Being open about personal problems
- Believing what you are told without checking facts
- Having difficulty saying no or confronting undesirable behavior

The authors qualify this list by saying that many of these qualities are good ones welcomed in the free world; however, they potentially spell trouble when dealing with offenders. People who possess these qualities should be especially aware of the possibility that they could be manipulated.

Officers need to know themselves and be aware of their strengths and weaknesses. If you see yourself at risk, according to this scale, or your supervisor or others have warned you, heed these warnings. Regularly review your perceptions and behavior with a trusted professional. Having firm guidelines and always following them will help prevent your falling victim to the con artist.

DEALING WITH DIFFICULT PEOPLE

Most probation officers have at least one or two probationers they dread seeing. These are people who are angry at the world and difficult to talk to, or folks who complain nonstop so that it is difficult to ask even the most basic questions. Even otherwise pleasant people can be difficult when they are on probation. New officers may think they can force a probationer into the proper demeanor by talking loudly or roughly. This technique generally does not work as desired and may backfire.

When dealing with difficult people, the first thing the officer should do is try to understand what the probationer is feeling and why. Many people mask fear by being rude or defiant. Some probationers are afraid and do not want the officer to know. They may have had some bad experiences with other officers. You may know that you are honest and fair, but a new client just reporting to you does not know that and may have no frame of reference to expect such a thing. Some probationers are very angry over real or imagined injustices done to them elsewhere. Some will have prejudices about the officer due to race, gender, or other factors. Some are humiliated at being in the system and only can respond in anger.

As a professional, the officer must refuse to accept any of the probationer's behaviors as personal attacks. Instead, the officer must consider the possible sources of the hostility and proceed in a detached, no-nonsense fashion. It may be necessary to advise probationers that their hostility and anger have been noted and are not helpful, but generally, only time will break down these kinds of barriers. Lectures are usually futile.

Here are some tips for diffusing difficult people:

- *Listen.* The best way to calm angry persons is to listen until they are talked out.
- *Repeat.* Repeat what you heard so they know you are listening and got it right. If you misunderstand, they can correct you.
- *Speak softly.* Although there is a school of thought which teaches that the way to manage anger is to match tone and volume, these folks are in the minority. In corrections, the speak softly/carry a big stick approach is better.
- *Ask them what they want.* Offenders have needs and wants that probation cannot always meet. Ask them anyway what it is they expect from the system or from you as the officer. Sometimes they have legitimate requests that can be honored. If not, the officer must tell the offender why. This goes a long way toward winning the probationer's cooperation. Often we write plans for our people

without knowing what they really think or want. It is very empowering to be asked, and probationers need to be empowered to take control over their lives in a positive way.

Do not let a difficult situation between you and a probationer become personal. Remember, they usually are reacting to your position, not to you personally. Probation officers are not necessarily going to be well liked. Those with an overwhelming need for universal acceptance should look for another profession. With time and experience, officers are less vulnerable to verbal attacks from their clients. Maintaining the professional barriers described earlier and following a pre-set code of behavior can insulate the officer from being manipulated, conned, or angered by probationers who are masters at this.

KEY POINTS TO REMEMBER

The reader should be able to discuss each of the following items:

- There are five types of officers and a competent professional employs skills and traits from each.
- Use formal titles and last names.
- Hold only business conversations.
- Reveal no personal information about yourself or other officers.
- Notify your supervisor when a probationer has a connection to your private life.
- Confront sexual/romantic proposals immediately and say no.
- Avoid personal relationships with families of probationers.
- Avoid doing business with probationers.
- Monitor your own risk level for manipulation.
- Defuse tense or difficult situations.

Handling The Stickies

A s previously stated, it is imperative that probation officers remember that they are dealing in human services and treat their probationers with courtesy and respect. Most of the offenders you supervise will respond appropriately to fair treatment. Although they may never share your value system, they can learn to follow the conditions of probation and abide by departmental polices. Many of your clients will complete probation successfully and never reoffend. If they show up in your church or neighborhood in a few years, you will be pleased with their achievements.

There are, however, a few probationers whose behavior is so disruptive or unacceptable that it must be addressed. These are the "stickies." Although there are many different personality types and endless behavior patterns, some seem to repeat themselves with great frequency among probationers.

The Constant Complainer

Perhaps the most common problem offender is the constant complainer. Some sources describe this as the "victim" mentality. Whatever you choose to call them, these individuals frequently show up in probation offices and are so irritating that officers everywhere groan when they see the constant complainer coming. The constant complainers believe that they are the victims and consistently blame others for their problems. If they admit they committed an offense, they will immediately justify it by saying that they "were hanging with the wrong crowd" or make a similar excuse.

These offenders seem to thrive on crisis and will present a new disaster each time they report. In some cases, they are genuinely distraught due to the perpetual chaos of their lives. Sometimes offenders use the crisis created by their own poor life management skills as an excuse to avoid responsibility. The constant complainer will be very adept at distracting the officer from the business at hand. Officers must learn to assess the immediate danger in any perceived crisis. Often, there is nothing to be done but listen, and then the offenders can be redirected to their probation issues.

Reality-based techniques are good for the constant complainers. They must be confronted with how their behavior has an impact on their lives and be held accountable for viable solutions. The officer always must be on guard against falling for a "poor me" attitude. Although some of these clients are very sympathetic characters, pity and sympathy do not bring change. Part of the officer's responsibility is to help empower the offenders to start constructive action to solve their own problems. When dealing with constant complainers, officers should listen, offer them a tissue, and keep moving forward with the interview. These probationers cannot be allowed to slide with excuses. They require firm guidelines and prompt action for noncompliance. It may be necessary to say "Mrs. Jones, I know your husband isn't working, but this is your probation and you need to make a restitution payment by the tenth or I will have to notify the court." This indicates that you are aware of the probationers' problems, but still hold them accountable to fulfill their conditions of probation.

Constant complainers need to be encouraged about their successes. Success breeds more success. They may need to recount their thought processes and actions in past crises to see that they always have alternatives and choices in any situation. Do not accept an attitude of "There's nothing I can do." Keep bringing them back to the issue at hand and ask them to list their options and analyze each one. Do not allow them to run on about how badly someone is treating them; instead, ask them what they intend to do about it. Constant complainers are not only irritating, they are self-destructive.

The "Good" Probationers

The "good" probationers or "good guys" identify with their officer. They will play up areas of commonality and talk in a "we versus them" manner. They are overly solicitous of the officer's welfare, ideas, and opinions. They may offer to do favors for the officer and always know where the best deals in town can be found. They have seen the error of their ways and spend a lot of time assuring the officer that they will be model probationers. In fact, they do not like to think of themselves as probationers and are offended by being thought of as criminals. These clients even may try to avoid reporting when other probationers are in the office due to embarrassment at being seen.

Good probationers like to flatter the officer. They may tell you that you are the best officer in the county or that no one else has ever been able to help them. These kinds of comments should be a warning. You may be an excellent officer, but it is just as possible that your probationer is trying to manipulate you. These people may border on being downright unctuous, and if so, they are easily recognized. Others are much smoother in their flattery, but their purpose is the same—to distract you from the business at hand. Turn away such compliments and immediately focus the probationers on their court orders, late payments, substance abuse problems, or other issues. It is perfectly acceptable to say

"Thanks, but there are lots of good officers here and your behavior does not depend on your officer, anyway. Now, when are you going to complete your community service?"

Among the good guy probationers are those who have been born again. Every officer has someone who claims to have experienced a miraculous spiritual conversion and only wants to talk about how changed he or she is. These offenders may not like any reference to their offense and insist that the past is over and not important. Officers will need to acknowledge the spiritual experience verbally and privately hope it is genuine. Then, they must keep the offenders focused on the idea that consequences for bad behavior do not just go away because they were converted. True repentance will lead to changed behavior. Officers should look for these behavioral changes and not be distracted by rhetoric.

Other good guy probationers are substance abusers who have sobered up and only want to talk about their treatment. Like the born agains, they may sound good, but consistent, improved behavior is the measuring line in probation. Do not be dazzled by verbiage. Behavior is what counts. Reporting regularly and in a timely manner, keeping current on probation payments, working, supporting the family, and maintaining sobriety are concrete measures of behavior. Regardless of what the probationers say, their behavior must meet these basic expectations. They need to "walk the talk."

THE SEDUCER/SEDUCTRESS

Seductive behavior can occur with either gender and can be directed at either gender. The seductive probationer uses sex appeal to manipulate people. These individuals subtly and overtly will approach officers and set them up for involvement. When caught, they usually deny they were doing anything wrong or claim that they were not serious. This behavior is sometimes subconscious, but it still must be addressed. Let the offenders know in no uncertain terms that their behavior is not welcomed and will not be tolerated. Document any incidents or inappropriate comments and let the offenders know you are doing so. This sends a clear message that you are not just demurring, you mean business. If the offenders realize that you have alerted someone else to their behavior, they are less likely to continue it and become threatening.

Be on the alert for side comments, which appear to be innocuous but may not be. Unless offenders are on probation for a sex offense, there is usually no need to discuss their sex life. If the offenders try to open this door, the officer should take care to examine the motives behind it. Offenders may repeat someone else's inappropriate comments about the officer. They are testing the officer for vulnerability. Do not ignore this behavior either. Make the offenders know that you are not interested and will not allow this to continue. These probationers usually will abandon their advances if forced to, and you then can deal with their probation.

THE ANGRY PROBATIONER

Everyone has a few "tough" people on their caseload. These individuals are mad at the world. They come in sullen and uncommunicative or like to raise their voices at the officer and challenge everything. Occasionally, these people are even threatening. In most instances, they are not a danger to the officer, but they have learned that aggressive behavior intimidates people and they can get by this way. A few are dangerous and officers never should ignore the possibility for violence when dealing with any probationer.

Matching these offenders' volume for volume usually does not work. It is easy to allow yourself to become angry over the abusive tones they use and the things they may say, but officers can learn to control their emotional reactions to such behavior. Most of this is not personally aimed at the officer, but is typical behavior for the offender and may be their only coping mechanism.

When dealing with the angry offender, try to allow them to vent without interruption. Do not argue or threaten while this is occurring. Your response must be intellectual, not emotional. Listen to them and measure your responses. When the offenders calm down, let them know that you want to hear what they have to say, but that loud, abusive language will not be tolerated. See if you can get them to agree to slow down, tone down, and omit the verbal abuse. This is not the time for sermons about how offensive their language is; just give them some guidelines. Included in the guidelines should be an agreement that the offender will stay seated and not invade the officer's space.

This method will allow you to gain control over the offender who deliberately uses the tough person act to intimidate. It can diffuse persons who are truly angry and upset by letting them know that you will listen and might be an advocate. Everyone needs to be heard.

If your efforts to calm the offenders do not succeed, and you see their behavior escalating or believe you are in danger, excuse yourself and go for help. Often, the presence of another person in the room will encourage irate probationers to get themselves under control. It is best to go for your supervisor. Probationers may recognize the higher degree of authority and may respond better to someone they see as "in charge." As always, document such incidents, keeping in mind that this documentation may be needed in court someday.

Other tough people are those who are sarcastic or who refuse to talk to the officer beyond grunting "yes" or "no" answers. This behavior is a game designed to humiliate or frustrate the officer. Do not play. Make sure all questions are open ended and require more than yes or no answers. Some offenders have justification for not trusting anyone, and their probation officer is no exception. With time, these people can learn to be more communicative and more cooperative. It usually is not productive to attack this behavior at your first meeting, but eventually you will have to address it with the offender and, as always, document it in the file. Like anger, once you know the source of this resistance, it is easier to find ways to work around this.

ANTISOCIAL PERSONALITIES

There is much good literature available regarding those with antisocial personality disorders and probation officers should familiarize themselves with this personality type. (*See*, for example, Boyd Sharp's *Changing Criminal Thinking: A Treatment Program*.) In 1957, the American Psychiatric Association described psychopaths as "persons whose behavior is predominantly amoral or antisocial and characterized by impulsive, irresponsible actions satisfying only immediate and narcissistic interests without concern for obvious and implicit social consequences, accompanied by minimal outward evidence of anxiety or guilt." Today, the term *psychopath* is primary reserved for extreme cases such as Charles Manson, and has been replaced with the antisocial label (Robinson and Little, 1997).

Such a disorder seems to afflict all probationers, but this is not true. Those with antisocial personality disorder form a small percent of the general population, though such types are found much more frequently among offenders, especially those incarcerated. A study by Kessler, McGonagle, et al, (cited by Robinson and Little) indicates the incidence in the general population to be 3.5 percent, increasing to 3.7 to 4 percent when institutionalized persons are included. About 2.7 percent of the U.S. population is under some type of criminal justice supervision. Drs. Robinson and Little believe that the majority of these individuals suffer from some degree of antisocial personality disorder.

Probation officers should take care about assuming a diagnosis and labeling their clients as antisocial. These antisocial individuals are different from others in their lack of remorse or guilt about how they have harmed others. They can fake these things if necessary, but they do not really feel emotions as others do. Those with the antisocial personality disorder may display other personality disorders as well, so that it may be difficult to truly identify them. Probation officers do not have to diagnose deviant personality types. Other professionals are dedicated to this and may be more qualified to do so.

However, officers who suspect they are dealing with clients with an antisocial personality should review their own training and departmental polices. Such clients are often very bright and highly manipulative. An officer easily can find these offenders in control of interviews and casework. The best protection is to follow procedures. Always verify everything a probationer tells you, regardless of their personality type. Never break the rules, and only make exceptions according to departmental criteria. Do not get involved in a personal relationship with any probationer. Document everything.

No matter what probationer you are dealing with, always remember that as an officer, you have the power of the court behind you. It is not the officer's responsibility to force people to change. You cannot frighten, bully, coerce, or coax people into compliance. Probationers will change or not based on a complicated assortment of factors. No matter how difficult a client decides to be, the officer must remain professional. Attempts to undermine the officer are not personal; they are often in rebellion against authority of any kind. Angry people are not usually mad at their officer, although they will take their anger out on the officer. Seductive people have learned that seduction works for them and everyone is a target, including their probation officer. If you find yourself unable to manage a problem offender, discuss the case with your supervisor or a trusted coworker. We can learn a lot from each other, and other officers may have excellent tips for confronting and breaking through negative behaviors.

KEY POINTS TO REMEMBER

The reader should be able to discuss each of the following items:

- The clients' behavior towards you is not personal.
- Manage your own emotional reactions to bad behavior.
- Always confront and rebuff sexual proposals or innuendos.
- Do not get into shouting matches.
- Never make exceptions outside departmental guidelines.
- Do not take responsibility for the offender's behavior.
- Do take responsibility for faithfully executing your duties.
- Document everything.

Officer Safety:
Some Fundamentals

A lthough crime statistics tell us that crime rates are down (26 percent between 1993 and 1999), we live in a society in which daily we are bombarded by violent images. Our perception is that the world is an increasingly dangerous place, regardless of what statistics show. All persons have concerns about their personal safety. For corrections and law enforcement personnel who spend their waking hours among criminals, this is an even greater concern. Perhaps the most important thing probation officers can do to protect themselves is to remember who the clients are. Officers never can forget that probationers are criminals. Criminals operate in a different world from law-abiding citizens, and that world can be dangerous. It is possible to treat people with courtesy and respect and still protect oneself. Probation officers must make certain cautious behaviors habits and not deviate from them.

SOME BASICS

Probation officers should not give out personal information about themselves. There is no reason for an offender to need your address. Keep this information private. Even if agency or department practices call for officers to list their phone numbers, you can have your address omitted from the telephone directory by notifying the phone company. If your department allows, get an unlisted phone number as well or list your phone in another name, unknown to your probationers. This will protect you and your family from unpleasant or threatening phone calls at all hours. Do not respond to requests for information from city directories or "crisscross" directories. Check with your supervisor or human resource director about limiting public access to your address and other personal data. Some states have laws protecting public employees, and it may be possible to have this information withheld from the general public.

Probation officers should take care not to leave personal mail out in the office where probationers can see it. Some people take their bills to work to pay during the lunch hour and leave them on the desk in plain view. This mail may contain not only your address, but account numbers, which probationers could use to steal from you or perpetrate a fraud. If you like to write your bills at work, be sure to shred any sensitive information or take it home to destroy. In some departments, probationers are performing building maintenance and your own probationers could show up emptying your trash. If you address personal correspondence at work, do not mail it from the office. Often letters sit in an out box or on a secretary's desk overnight, giving ample time for any interested observer to jot down your address.

To illustrate the ease with which offenders can obtain and use personal information, consider the following true case. In a high school office, time cards for all employees were kept next to the time clock in plain view and within reach of anyone who entered the office. Names and Social Security numbers were clearly visible. A seventeen-year-old student used this information from the principal's card along with his address and phone number obtained from the telephone directory to establish credit at several department stores. The victim was unaware of the fraud until collection agencies began to call him. Many of your probationers will be much more sophisticated than this seventeen-year-old girl. Protect yourself.

As previously noted, officers should not discuss their marital status, children, or personal habits with probationers. Some of your clients will be stalkers or pedophiles who will remember all the details that they have learned about you and your family. You also will want to be careful about displaying family photos. The location may be so easily identifiable that your probationers could find your house by the photo. Living arrangements may be discernible from photos and provide probationers with information about you, your family, or your possessions. As previously discussed, probationers already know your work schedule, so they know when your family is home alone, or when your house is likely to be empty. A female officer living alone could put herself in jeopardy by things revealed from innocent photographs.

Most people take the same route to and from work daily. We tend to go the shortest or quickest route, making us easy to track and anticipate. Officers should be aware of surrounding traffic and vary their routes to avoid being an easy target. Park in a secure, well-lighted area. If you arrive at work before daylight or stay after dark, make arrangements to walk with someone to and from your car. Lock up your car and never leave valuables in view. When you return to your car, check the area around it for hiding places as you approach. Look inside to be sure there is no one waiting inside the vehicle. Have your keys ready and when you get in, lock the doors immediately.

In the Office

Although most assaults against probation officers occur on home visits, the probation office is the second highest site for attack (21 percent of attacks occur there according to a 1984 federal probation study cited in *Officer Safety: Strategies for Survival* (1993)). Follow regular office hours and never meet with a probationer after-hours without supervisory approval. Always have another officer present for after-hours meetings. Although you want to be flexible and considerate of your probationers' scheduling needs, you cannot forget who they are and take risks with your own safety.

The office itself should be arranged as safely as possible with an exit available for emergencies. As discussed earlier, try to set up your office so that a probationer cannot get between you and the door. Do not turn your back to the door. Although you may have no control over this, doors should open outward as recommended in the *Handbook On Probation Services/Guidelines for Probation Practice and Management*. (Klaus, 1998). Never allow a client to close the door. The officer should control the door and the locking mechanism. Some officers are working behind solid wood or steel doors. If attacked, they could be injured seriously before anyone could get keys or break down the door. Probationers who walk in and immediately close the door may be trying to gain control over the interview or intimidate the officer, and this cannot be allowed. Instruct the probationer to leave the door open and have a seat. During the interview, if you decide that the issues are too sensitive to be overheard, you may get up and close the door, but the offender should not have that power.

Probation offices are full of criminals, many of whom steal. Officers should have a permanent place for their purses, wallets, and other personal valuable items. These items should be secured in the same place every day on arriving at work. Keep your keys on your person and do not leave the office without them. Do not leave valuables unlocked in the office even for a quick trip to the copier. Sometimes offenders will show up in the hallway unattended, and they easily can ransack drawers or rifle through purses in the time it takes to walk to the lobby and back. If it is necessary to leave a probationer alone in the office, lock all files and valuables before leaving. This may seem awkward, and you may not want to insult your probationer by appearing distrustful. Yet, it is better to err on the side of caution in such instances. Perform this motion as unobtrusively as possible. Remember, probationers usually are accustomed to security measures. If they question you about it, simply state that it is your policy to always secure the desk and files whenever you leave the room. If your department has such a policy, so much the better.

In the Field

Field visits continue to be the subject of an ongoing debate in probation. After a decade of limiting home visits and labeling entire neighborhoods as too dangerous to visit, the tide may be turning. A number of critical incidents have caused the probation profession to concentrate on the issue of community involvement, including field visits.

As we mentioned, Jeffery Dahmer was already on probation when his neighbors began to complain about the odor emanating from his apartment, but his probation officer never had smelled anything because he never had made a field visit to Dahmer's residence. His department had deemed the neighborhood too dangerous for officers to enter. In August 1999, when Buford Furrow Jr. opened fire on a day care center and also murdered a postal worker in a separate incident, he was on probation, but he had never surrendered his guns, according to a court order.

Such incidents remind us of the importance of field visits. The Manhattan Institute, in an extensive survey of probation (*see* comments by Evans, 1999 and Arola and Lawrence, 1999) recommends that officers get out of the office and into the field. Around the country, projects focusing on community involvement such as Boston's Operation Night Light (Arola and Lawrence, 1999) are reporting some success. In his list of what works, Paul Gendreau (Latessa, 1999) names disruption of the criminal network as an important approach. Officers working in the actual neighborhoods where their probationers live are more likely to have an impact on the criminal network than those who supervise from a remote office.

Yes, field visits can be dangerous. On field visits, probation officers always should take precautions whether they are going into a high-crime area or to another neighborhood. The presence of a probationer in a neighborhood can make it a dangerous place regardless of how nice it appears. Officers who are authorized to carry weapons may tend to rely on their firearm too much. In a conversation with the author, Ed Read, a Supervising U.S. Probation Officer, stresses to his staff that they are "never to go anywhere with a weapon that they wouldn't go without."

Advance preparation before going out will save lost time and help ensure officer safety. Know where you are going. Have a map and good directions. Dress comfortably in clothes and shoes you can run in, if necessary. Avoid wearing expensive jewelry or clothing that draws attention to you. Female officers should lock their purses in the office or the trunk of their car and carry only badge, keys, and cell phone.

Everyone should leave an itinerary before departing on field visits. If your department does not have a policy about checking in on field visits, agree with your supervisor or clerical staff about what your practice will be. It is a good idea to call the office when you arrive at a residence and again when you depart. Probationers need to know that someone is aware of your presence in their home or neighborhood. Carry a cell phone, if available, and ask for one if your department does not regularly issue them. Try to combine your home visits with another officer and make field visits together. This is safer, and working in teams often produces more information than you can obtain working alone. If your department allows, learn to use pepper spray and carry it with you at all times. If your jurisdiction permits probation officers to be armed, be sure you are properly trained and follow department guidelines for carrying, using, and storing your weapon.

Probation officers may hope to "catch" their probationers doing something wrong. Although actually catching a probationer in the act of a violation is good evidence, it also can be dangerous. If you are making unannounced visits, remember that you could be walking into a drug deal or a shooting. Be aware of your surroundings. Before you get out of the car, scan the area carefully for suspicious activity, including people or cars that do not belong there. If you are not sure what is going on, drive around the block and scan the area again. If you have a cell phone, you may be able to call your probationers and have them meet you at the door. As you exit your vehicle, scan the area one more time to be sure that your path is clear. Lock your car unless you expect to make a hasty exit.

When approaching the door of a residence, stand to the side of the door while you knock or ring the bell. If there is an intoxicated or deranged person on the other side with a gun, you are less likely to be shot if you move away from the door. When the door is opened, quickly scan the interior before entering. If the room is full of people you do not know or they appear to be intoxicated, do not enter. Some residences are so dark that you cannot see who is inside or what is going on. Do not enter these premises. Ask your probationer to come outside to talk to you.

Never enter a residence without being invited. Your probationer or a family member later could claim that you entered without permission, and this might negate any evidence you find. Juvenile officers generally will not want to enter a residence if no adult is present. Also, do not enter a residence just because someone calls out "Come in." You have no way of knowing who that person is or what is on the other side of the door. Identify yourself and ask them to come to the door to talk to you.

Officers need to be careful about being caught alone in a residence with someone of the opposite sex or someone who has a history of violent or irrational behavior. Knowing your clients can help you know whether it is safe to visit with them alone. If you know your probationer's family and living habits, you can better judge when other people will be present. If you are uncomfortable being alone with probationers in their home, take a partner with you, or discuss with your supervisor other ways to fulfill your field visit requirements. Do not ignore your instinct that something is dangerous. After a while, experienced officers will develop very sensitive and accurate instincts about such things. Use common sense and be cautious.

Some residences will be dirtier than you imagined possible. You will be uncomfortable there and perhaps afraid to sit down. These are natural reactions. It is not the officer's place to make the probationer feel good. If it is not safe or sanitary, do not sit down. Do not accept food or drink on a field visit. This makes it into a social occasion, and your visits are not social. There is always the danger (however remote) that someone could put something in your food or drink. A polite "No thank you" is sufficient.

Field visits can be fruitless because there is so much noise and confusion in the home. In such cases, you have some options. Advise your probationers that you need to discuss something with them in a quiet atmosphere. If you feel free to do so, ask them to turn off the television or stereo, or ask if there is another room where you can talk without so much distraction. If this is not possible, instruct your probationer to come to your office to discuss the problem. Give them an appointment time, preferably the next working day. Say something like "Mr. Jones, we need a quiet time to discuss your AA work. Can you come see me at 8:30 tomorrow morning?" Remember that sometimes noise and confusion are indicative of how your probationer lives and you will find the same situation any time you visit. However, some probationers may create extra confusion and chaos to avoid talking to you. By scheduling an office visit immediately in such circumstances, your probationer is not able to distract you from the business at hand.

If a probationer or someone else at the residence becomes belligerent or threatening during a visit, excuse yourself and get out immediately. If you have stayed close to the door, you can do this quickly and with some grace. Do not be concerned that the probationer will feel they "ran you off." Say something like "I see this is not a good time. Please excuse me and I'll talk to you about this another time." Document the incident and discuss with your supervisor how to proceed. You may want to call or write the probationer to schedule a special office visit or you may just want to discuss the incident at their next reporting date. Some threats will require that you file charges or notify the court. The important thing is to be safe and not to continue being in a potentially dangerous situation.

In some jurisdictions, officers make field visits with probationers at neutral locations if the probationer's neighborhood is deemed too dangerous for officers to visit. This seems to defeat the primary purpose of a field visit, which is to see the probationer's living situation. If a residence is so dangerous that you cannot visit there, field visits lose meaning. Carefully analyze the purpose of your field visits to determine if enough is gained to justify continuing them when you cannot go to a probationer's home.

Many departments have policies that provide criteria for waiving field visits. If yours does not, tell your supervisor that you wish to discontinue field visits with a specific probationer and list the reasons why. "It's a terrible neighborhood" is not a sufficient reason. This is subjective. Your supervisor may not think it is such a bad neighborhood at all and may have family or friends living there.

Reasons to stop field visits to a location should include this type of information:

- Recent shootings on that street
- Sightings of drug trafficking

- Presence of other known offenders at or near the location
- History of violence by your probationer or others at the location
- Groups of people drinking at or near the residence
- Verbal threats toward officers working in the area
- Incidents of vandalism to officers' vehicles in the area

List the dates and times of these occurrences. If someone in the household has threatened you, report this at once to your supervisor. If other officers have experienced similar problems, include their statements with your request.

The information obtained from field visits is helpful, and there is some deterrent factor at work when offenders know their officer may show up at any time. However, the advantages gained by field visits are not worth risking your safety. If it is too dangerous, say so and document this in the probationer's file.

A final word on field visits—unless you are working surveillance, do not make field visits after dark without advising your supervisor, and always have another officer with you. Friday afternoons and holidays also can be bad times in the field since many people may be drinking and drugging. Plan these visits well, notify your supervisor of your destination, and take another officer with you.

TRANSPORTING

Officers may have occasion to transport probationers and be in the car alone with them. In some jurisdictions or departments, this is common practice. Usually this is okay, but sometimes it is foolish or downright dangerous. If you need to transport someone, consider the offender's history—both criminal and mental. Has the offender ever made threats to an officer or acted inappropriately with an officer? What is the neighborhood like where you are going? How long will you be in the car together? If you have a "gut" feeling that this is dangerous, do not transport without a partner. The so-called "gut" feeling may be an accurate instinct for survival or just common sense based on past experience with the probationer. In either case, take heed and take precautions.

Males should not transport female probationers without a chaperone. In many cases, female officers should not transport male probationers alone. Anytime you believe your probationer is agitated and could become violent, or you are driving to a dangerous or unknown area, take another officer and be sure to notify your supervisor of your intentions. The potential for a probationer to direct you to an isolated area and attack you may be remote, but it does exist. Know where you are going and get directions from a map or another officer.

In Harm's Way

Many probationers are angry at the world in general and the criminal justice system in particular. They may be mentally unbalanced or under the influence of drugs or alcohol. Probationers may be of a different race or gender from the officer and have misconceptions about your behavior and motives. Officers may be weary of excuses and bad behavior. When these two mind-sets meet, there is the potential for conflict.

Probationers are people who could not or would not obey the law. They may continue to ignore what the judge ordered them to do. They may be rude or disrespectful to the officer. Some of their behavior may be foolish, dangerous, or vulgar. Probation officers must refrain from reacting to such behaviors and proceed to carry out their duties in a professional manner. Do not match anger for anger, and do not take insults as personal attacks. As a representative of the court or the probation department, you have nothing to prove.

When dealing with angry probationers, do not let them draw you into a shouting match. Make it a practice to listen to what people are saying and trying to say. The probationer's anger is sometimes a cover for fear and frustration. Probationers may stop being rude once they know you are listening to them. Others are trying to bait their officer into unprofessional conduct. Do not allow a probationer to control you this way. Their attacks are rarely personal unless you have allowed the relationship to become personal. Practice keeping the volume of your voice low and your tone neutral. Stick to the facts when meeting with irate or unstable probationers. Opinions or assumptions are not useful and only will anger them more. Keep your hands in plain view so that they do not think you are reaching for a weapon.

A probationer who feels you are personally the enemy is more likely to hurt you than one who sees you as just someone doing a job. Most probationers will be able to recognize fair and consistent behavior, but they will not tolerate what they think is demeaning or abusive treatment. When dealing with an angry probationer, limit the use of the "I" word. Refer to the court or the probation department. Statements such as "I'm going to have to send you to jail" make things seem personal and create enemies. In truth, probation officers do not have the power to send anyone to jail, they only can recommend. When delivering bad news to your probationer say something like "Mr. Jones, I'll have to notify the court of this violation, and we'll see what the judge wants to do." This does not sound like a personal vendetta by the officer, and it places the final outcome on the court.

When you have done all you can do to de-escalate a situation with angry probationers and they continue to appear dangerous or threatening, excuse yourself and get a supervisor. Many probationers immediately will start to calm down in front of a higher authority figure. In cases where your probationer has a problem with your age, gender, or race, asking in a third party may help bring the situation under control so that you can finish your meeting.

Although it may not be natural to sit quietly while someone verbally abuses you, there are times when it can be the wisest choice. Officers who are not perceived as the enemy are in less danger and can get more cooperation from their probationers. Some deranged people may go home to get their gun and return to take their revenge on the last person who made them angry. Keep your contacts with probationers on a professional level. This avoids many hassles, much anxiety, and, of course, much danger.

LOVE, INFATUATION, AND THE SEXUALLY AGGRESSIVE PROBATIONER

Some probationers will fixate on their officer as a romantic object. This can be dangerous if you do not understand what is happening. You must address this situation immediately. Some probationers are mentally ill and will fantasize about their officer. They may bring themselves to believe that their feelings are reciprocated. There also will be some narcissistic probationers who think that everyone they meet is in love with them or wants them sexually, and they include their probation officer in that misconception.

Officers can prevent a lot of heartache and trouble by monitoring their own behavior to be sure it is always professional and businesslike. The observance of titles and last names helps in this regard. Handshakes are okay; other touching is not. Do not pat your probationers on the back, touch their hand or hug them. These behaviors are not consistent with the role of a court officer or a corrections officer. Sick or vulnerable people will read more into such contact and believe your interest in them is more than professional.

Do not do favors for probationers, and do not use the word *favors*. Some probationers will interpret this as meaning that you really are doing them a favor because you have a "special" relationship. Officers generally are allowed great flexibility in scheduling appointments and making recommendations to the court. When you agree to allow a probationer to report or pay late, you may be acting within the authority granted you by the court and according to departmental guidelines. The probationer, however, may not see it this way. If your probationer asked you for a "big personal favor" to be allowed to skip his or her payment this month, the individual may see this as a personal favor and not routine discretion on your part. If the probationers are unbalanced, they may perceive your "favor" as an indication of your romantic interest. Always remind your probationers that you do not do favors. If any exceptions are made, let them know that they will be according to departmental guidelines, not due to any personal feelings on your part. This is a small thing that can become a big thing if not corrected.

Personal remarks directed to you about your appearance, lifestyle, or marital status must be examined closely. Like sexual harassment issues, you need some common sense in this area. A probationer, who says you look very handsome or lovely today, just may be telling the truth or being polite. Say thank you and go on with the visit. Anything beyond that is questionable. Comments such as "Your wife sure is lucky to have a good looking man like you," or "Miss Jones, you sure do have some fine legs," are out of line. Ignoring such remarks allows some probationers to think that you welcome them. Others may think they intimidated you and use this to try and gain control over you. Neither of these scenarios is acceptable.

Address inappropriate compliments, remarks, or questions immediately. You might try responding with "Thanks, but we are not here to discuss me." If that does not work, you may need to be very assertive and say something like, "Miss Smith, I think that comment is inappropriate. Please do not talk to me that way again. We're here to discuss your probation, not me."

Questions about your personal life are also out of line and should be discouraged. Perhaps the most common two questions officers are ever asked about are marital status and parenthood. When asked if you are married or if you have children, feel free to respond with "Why are you asking me that? My personal life has nothing to do with your probation." Or, you may prefer something like "Yes, I am married, and that has nothing to do with your case." Keep these remarks civil and in good humor, but make it clear that your life is off limits.

Vulgar, suggestive remarks or noises are not to be tolerated ever. If this occurs, confront the probationer immediately, and document the incident as well. Most probationers will deny making any such remarks or noises even if it is obvious that they have. Be prepared to make your point and still allow the probationer some way to save face. You might say something like, "I guess my hearing is failing me because I know you did not really say what I just heard, and I know you will never say such a thing again." The offenders may admit what they said or did but insist they meant nothing by it. You then can remind them that serious or not, it was inappropriate, and you do not want it to happen again.

Do not ignore bad behavior and hope it will stop. Also, do not get angry or act shocked or afraid. Just name the behavior and state your expectations that it will not happen again. Except in rare cases, this approach will get you the results you need, and you will not have to repeat this scene.

Some people are natural flirts. Call it charisma or charm, some individuals just seem to get others going sexually. If you are experiencing frequent problems with your probationers in this area, take a look at your own behavior to see if you are inadvertently causing it. Ask your friends or another officer for their opinions. Flirting has no place on the job, especially in corrections. If you are interacting with your probationers on such a level, you need to be aware of this so that you can modify your behavior. You may know that you never actually would do anything wrong, but probationers are accustomed to breaking the rules and hope you will too. Mentally unbalanced people could become dangerous if they decide to take your "relationship" to another level.

Special Problems

If an offender shows up at your home, you think you are being followed, or if you are receiving harassing phone calls, take note of the
dates and times and document these. With caller ID and answering
machines, you may be able to trace calls. If you actually see one of your
probationers in your neighborhood or elsewhere in your private life,
note this. It may be an innocent coincidence, or your probationer may be
stalking you. Talk to your supervisor if you think you are being stalked.

Get Trained, Be Aware, Stay Alert

Being aware of risks and alert to your surroundings can eliminate
much danger at work and in your private life. There is excellent officer
safety training all over the country. Especially look for training geared to
the probation officer as opposed to law enforcement training. Federal
probation does a fine job of this, and this training is more appropriate for
the probation officer than police officer safety training. However,
probation officers who are peace officers also may need police officer
safety training.

When Prevention Is Not Enough

Even after practicing every safety measure available, some officers fall
victim to attack. Parsonage and Miller (1993) report career victimization
rates ranging from 38 percent in Pennsylvania to 55 percent in New York
State probation. Incidents may be actual assaults or threats and intimi-
dation. Corrections and law enforcement personnel have come to call
these *critical incidents*. A critical incident is one in which the individuals
feel vulnerable and overwhelmed. The individuals have lost control of
their circumstances, and may suffer an inability to function at the time of
the incident or subsequently. The critical incident usually is unexpected.
People who experience a critical incident may find that their basic beliefs

about how the world works are disrupted. Officers who have been through critical incidents also may experience long-term effects such as depression, anxiety, fear, inappropriate behaviors such as alcohol abuse, or physical symptoms and complaints.

Officer Safety: Strategies for Survival (1993) offers some suggestions for coping with the critical incident. These include:

- Engaging in strenuous physical exercise alternating with relaxation within the first forty-eight hours
- Staying busy
- Talking
- Spending time with other people
- Avoiding drugs or alcohol
- Sharing your feelings with others in a safe environment
- Keeping to your normal schedule, as much as possible
- Not making any major life decisions or changes
- Understanding that it is okay to feel bad and that thoughts or flashbacks will decrease with time

Since the entire department or office will be affected by one officer's critical incident, management should have procedures in place to deal with these. Debriefing teams are one good idea. Ensuring that the employees have their basic needs met and allowing flexible work schedules are also important. Counseling services should be available. While it is necessary to examine any critical incident, it is also important to avoid placing blame on the "victim." The entire department will be watching to see how management responds to such incidents, and morale can be enhanced or adversely impacted.

Most officers will recover from critical incidents and continue with their careers. Some will opt to leave after an incident. With proper training in prevention and a good support system in the event of an incident, more officers can recover and continue productive careers.

KEY POINTS TO REMEMBER

The reader should be able to discuss each of the following items:

- Keep personal data private.
- Arrange your office with an unobstructed exit.
- Secure valuables and keep keys on your person.
- Do not work alone after hours.
- Keep your office door open during a conference.
- Make field visits in pairs and take a phone with you.
- Be aware of your surroundings.
- Report anyone stalking you.
- Do not flirt and do not allow probationers to flirt with you.
- Seek out safety training appropriate for probation personnel.
- A critical incident need not mean the end of your career.

Office Etiquette

Good manners are always appropriate and good practice. They signal basic respect for other people as well as oneself. Certainly, professional people ought to be courteous to each other and the public, but for public servants, this is even more critical. It is also often more difficult due to the unpleasant nature of some probation duties. Officers who have memorized the criminal code and are the best writers in the department are handicapped if they cannot get along with people. Good manners can help.

HELLO, HELLO

One of the most basic elements of good manners is a proper greeting. As discussed in an earlier chapter, officers should define the rules for their probationers about how they wish to be addressed and treat probationers with the same courtesy. The use of a title and last name (Mr. Jones/Ms. Smith) is an important step toward establishing officer authority and receiving courteous treatment. It is more difficult to be rude when using formal titles and last names. Use formal titles and last names as a regular practice to protect yourself.

Most officers work in locations with secretaries or receptionists who first meet the probationers and have them sign in. Once notified that you have a probationer in the lobby, do not tell the secretary to "Send him on back." This not only is rude, but it is a security risk as well. Officers should meet their probationers in the lobby and escort them back to their office.

TO SHAKE OR NOT TO SHAKE

Establish a policy for yourself about whether you will offer a hand-shake to your probationers. Some officers are uncomfortable about this altogether or just with certain probationers. If you are one of these, make it your personal policy never to offer your hand to any client. This way you avoid favoritism and accusations of discrimination. If you offer your handshake to one probationer, you should do the same for the rest. Many offenders will extend their hand to you in greeting, and good manners requires that you respond with a handshake. Wash your hands a lot, and consider this part of good client relationships.

Handshake or not, greet you probationer with "Hello, Mr. Smith. Come on back to my office," and lead the way. Once in the office, ask your probationer to be seated. You may add a casual "How are you today?" as you get out the file. Unless the probationer appears distressed, proceed to the purpose of the current visit. Look at your probationers while they are talking and while you talk to them. It is rude to avoid looking at your clients. They may perceive this as fear on your part, which sends a message that they are in control of the relationship. The probationers may think someone who will not look at them is afraid to confront them. Looking at your client is good manners and a good control mechanism. Watch for body language. Remember, many offenders may lie to their officer. Watch for telltale signs of dishonesty.

Most people want others to look at them while they are talking, and some new officers may think they should demand this from probationers. While there are times to demand this, be careful before picking this fight. In some cultures, it is considered rude to look someone directly in the eye. Other offenders may be mentally disturbed and consider this flirtatious behavior on your part. Others may be threatened by it and become overtly hostile. You cannot supervise someone who will not communicate with you, and eye contact is a part of communication. However, this is a sensitive area, and officers should know their probationers and proceed with caution before making this an issue.

Although you must take notes on the information the probationer is giving you and any deadlines or agreements you make, keep these as brief as possible and try not to write while your probationer is talking. Jot down what you have to and after the client leaves, complete the chronological entry.

INTERRUPTIONS AND PRIVACY

Phone calls and other interruptions are distracting to you and unfair to the probationer. You may not have the luxury of having your calls held, but you can limit the length of calls and be sure to excuse yourself to the probationer when you have to answer the phone. Personal calls during an office visit are unprofessional and rude. Tell the caller that you have a client with you and cannot talk. Educate your family and friends about your duties and the best times to call if they must. Calls from the court always take precedence over anything, but calls from other officers or agencies should be kept brief. If at all possible, ask the caller to allow you to call back when you finish the current office visit. They may be asking for information that should not be discussed in front of a probationer.

If you must take sensitive calls during an office visit, ask your probationer to excuse you, escort the probationer to the lobby, and then take the call. Discourage office pals from barging in during office visits. To individuals who want to discuss lunch plans, respond with a statement such as this: "I can't make any plans right now. Let me get back to you after this office visit." This usually will send the message you want.

Some offices are so busy and noisy that you may want to close your door during office visits. As we discussed earlier, probation officers who work with adults should think twice about this. Although many probationers prefer to see you behind closed doors, it may not be the safest thing for you. Never allow the probationer to close the door. In doing so, they take control of the interview. If your door locks from the inside, you certainly do not want to allow the probationer to lock you in. A simple "Please leave the door open, Ms. Smith" will send your message and protect you against both physical threat and innuendo. Juvenile officers often are encouraged to conduct closed-door interviews due to the confidential nature of their work. In such circumstances, officers should have a parent or other witness present if there is any concern on their part about a physical threat or false accusations.

It is a good idea to keep a box of tissue on hand. Probationers often have things to cry about and although you cannot hug them, you can extend the kindness of handing them a tissue while they cry.

When the visit is over, be sure you give the probationers a new appointment card. Escort them to the lobby and say goodbye. When you return to your office, make the chronological entry and put away the file. Letting these stack up will lead to confusion, and important facts may get lost.

Company

Some probationers bring friends, children, or other relatives with them to report. In the case of children, it may be that the offender has no suitable childcare and has no choice. It is also possible that the probationer does this deliberately to ensure a shortened visit and keep you from drug testing or asking too many difficult questions. Probationers fearing arrest may bring children to postpone the inevitable.

Be straightforward and tell your probationer if the children are distracting you from the work you both need to be doing. Ask what other childcare arrangements can be made, and reschedule the appointment for that time. If they insist there is no other option, and they allow their children to run around the office and play with the items on your desk, tell the children directly to stop and sit down. Often children will respond to your authority long enough for you to finish your visit. You also may try scheduling a home visit to finish your interview with the understanding that the probationer can give you his or her undivided attention at that time.

Sometimes probationers report in the company of another offender. This is a violation in most jurisdictions and must be addressed. Some probationers may say they do not know this is a violation. Others know, but are hoping you will not notice or confront it. Do not allow other probationers or offenders to sit in on your visit unless you need information from them. Do not address this in the lobby, but when the probationer is in your office, advise them of this violation, and tell them that you are noting in their file their continuing association with known offenders. Instruct them not to repeat this behavior. Ask them if they can make other arrangements to get home, and notify the other individual's officer.

Probationers do not exist in a vacuum and their friends and family sometimes can be very helpful to an officer. It is also true that probationers will bring other people to report with them for a variety of reasons that are not helpful or acceptable to the officer. Always consider the possibility that the probationer is trying to distract or intimidate you. Determine the relationship of the person they are bringing and decide if that person will be allowed in your office. For instance, if you are supervising a female you suspect is being battered by her spouse, you may not want him sitting in on her visits. Sometimes parents want to accompany their adult children to the probation office. This may be helpful, or they may be enabling the offender. Many departments have well-defined policies about this, and you should know what they are. In any case, the officer controls the interview and who attends it—not the offender.

Physical Contact

In addition to the handshake, some probationers will try to have physical contact with their officer. This may be a pat on the back or a touch of the hand, but it is inappropriate and must not be allowed. It is possible that a probationer genuinely likes you and is responding to you as a human being. It is also possible that the probationer is trying to get control of your relationship and compromise you. Regardless of the motivation, the probationers must be confronted and told to stop immediately. If your department has a policy about this, it is easy to say "Mr. Jones, we have a policy about no physical contact between officers and probationers. Please do not do that." This usually will do the trick, but if the offenders "forget," remind them again and note the incident in the file if it continues. This could be a set up. Report to your supervisor if you believe this is happening or you think that you are being targeted.

Officers must be careful to avoid even the appearance of wrongdoing. A pat on the back of the hand from a probationer may be innocent, but it can be perceived quite differently by someone observing from the lobby. Establish a reputation for yourself as strictly professional so that people are not quick to believe false accusations if they ever arise. You should be able to say that it is your practice never to have physical contact with a probationer beyond the handshake.

Colleagues, Coworkers, and Peers

You will work with a lot of different officers, supervisors, court personnel, police, and other corrections/human services employees. Most of the people you will meet will be dedicated, smart, and hard working. Some will not be. The development of your professional demeanor and office etiquette will help you when dealing with these other professionals.

JUDGES

Probation officers are servants of the court. Judges run the courts and each judge is different. Judges have the authority to control who works for them and how their staff will dress, behave, and speak in court. If your department does not cover your judge's philosophy during orientation, be sure to ask your supervisor what the judge expects. The answer to a judge is almost always followed by the words "sir" or "ma'am." Whether you agree with a particular judge, the judge commands respect. Ask permission to speak to the judge. Have your information ready. If you do not know the answer to their question, say so and offer to get that information promptly.

If you work for a judge who likes to socialize with probation officers, be careful about participating in these events. If you go, stay sober and rest assured that what you say and do will not be "off the record." Never give your judge a reason to criticize your demeanor or attitude.

ATTORNEYS

Attorneys become judges. Attorneys represent your probationers in revocations. Attorneys who were prosecutors become defense lawyers. Exciting as it is to meet at the local bar, think this over carefully. As with judges, anything you say or do will be remembered.

Attorneys sometimes attack witnesses, including probation officers. This is not personal, but part of the attorney's job. Just as when you talk to the judge, have your information ready. Be sure it is accurate. Say only what you know for fact, and admit when you do not know something. Maintain a professional demeanor even under cross-examination.

OTHER COURT PERSONNEL

Respect also should be extended to your judge's staff. Court administrators, clerks, and bailiffs have close relationships with the judges, and they can be your best friend or your worst enemy. Treat these people courteously and respect their proximity to the judge. They may be able to give you sound advice about what your judge wants, and they can expedite your access to the judge. They have the judge's ear all day; you have it occasionally for five minutes.

YOUR BOSS

Whether you have the boss from hell or boss of the year, the boss is still the boss. Although there are times when a supervisor mistreats an employee, most employee grievances are not over mistreatment, but the enforcement of rules and policy. Know your department's policy and police yourself so that the supervisor does not have to do so. Ask how your supervisor wants certain things done. As long as the supervisor's methods are legal and proper, you need to follow his or her instructions.

Supervisors really are people, too. They appreciate common courtesy. If your boss likes officers to stop by just to say good morning or good night, do it. This is a small thing that indicates your respect for their position and willingness to go along. The assessment of an employee's attitude is an arbitrary thing. Do not give anyone ammunition to accuse you of having a bad attitude or being uncooperative or hard to supervise. You can state your opinions and disagree with your supervisor in a civil manner without causing animosity. Watch the people who do this well, and learn from them.

YOUR PEERS

Although you may not respect some other officers' work or agree with their techniques, never let it show to the public. A condition in any code of ethics is common sense. There are times when it will be you (the probation officer) against them (the offenders). You must present a united front to maintain order and supervise your probationers. Everyone has met the probationer who wants to tell you how bad their last officer was. Do not allow this. Remember, offenders may lie to their officers. Even if you think the previous officer was negligent or made mistakes, do not say so to your probationers. Tell them that you do not want to discuss their former officer, but you do intend to correct any confusion or deficiencies immediately.

It is sometimes difficult to be friendly with coworkers you consider incompetent or lazy, but it is necessary to greet such people civilly when you meet them and extend them the same courtesy you would to anyone else. People change and situations change. The officer you once had disrespect for someday could be your partner or supervisor.

If you experience casework problems due to another officer, see your supervisor for assistance. The supervisor may tell you to fix it. If so, fix it. This is a good indication that the problems are long-standing and your supervisor is already aware. Management may be working on the problem without your knowledge. By "fixing it," you gain your supervisor's respect as someone they can count on to put the welfare of the probationer and the department ahead of personal grievances. If the officer you have difficulty with reports to a different supervisor, you still must report problems to your own. This is a proper chain of command, and using it is essential for the orderly functioning of the organization. It is improper for an officer to complain to another supervisor. Go to your own supervisor and let your supervisor handle it according to department procedure.

Bosom Buddies

Some officers will become your friends, and you will enjoy their company very much. Do not allow this to interfere with your workday, and do not discuss confidential information with them that they do not need to know. Keep your office behavior professional and do not allow personal conversations to go on within earshot of probationers. When you establish friendships at work, you may be opening the door for deeper relationships or even romance. Monitor your own behavior to avoid anything improper and be wary of office romances, which historically can be problematic. Your department may have a policy regarding this, and you should know it before embarking on a serious relationship with a coworker.

Romances between supervisors and subordinates are always risky. They easily can be misconstrued as sexual harassment and open the entire department up for lawsuits. Officers and supervisors should think long and hard before embarking on these kinds of relationships. It is improper for a supervisor to be linked romantically with someone they supervise directly. Even if the officer reports to another supervisor, these relationships can cause problems. An officer who is pressured by a supervisor should say no and get help according to the department policy. If department policy is unclear or ineffective, the county or state can assist. Sexual harassment is covered under federal law, so no one ever should have to tolerate improper treatment.

Clerical/Support Staff

People everywhere like to complain about their secretaries or other clerical and support staff. In a field like probation where most employees have degrees, the clerical staff can get a bad rap. Although there are bad secretaries, most are conscientious and anxious to support their officers. These employees should be treated with the same courtesy as fellow officers. Adding "please" and "thank you" to your requests will expedite their production. As mentioned in another chapter, giving them legible/intelligible instructions reduces a great deal of confusion and wasted time. When you do have problems with the clerical staff or other support personnel, notify your own supervisor, and let your supervisor take action. Although you outrank clerical and support personnel, you do not necessarily supervise them. As one chief pointed out, clerical staff do not have the freedom of movement enjoyed by officers. Whereas officers may find stress relief in traveling for field or court visits, and largely control their own schedules, clerical staff are pretty much locked into the office, and they work a more structured schedule. Consideration for them pays off in improved production and office morale.

OTHER AGENCIES

One of the big tests of your professional ability is your talent for networking with other professionals and other agencies. Many officers consider themselves brokers of services and practice making referrals to other human services agencies. All officers spend a great deal of time dealing with law enforcement and other corrections personnel. These contacts can enhance your casework and service delivery both to offenders and the community. There are many excellent collaborations across the country between or among various agencies. Find out from your supervisor which agencies your department uses and who the contact persons are.

Eventually you will encounter some sort of roadblock from another agency. Jails can leave you waiting for hours; police may not give you reports in a timely manner; mental health agencies may be slow to call you back. When you are working on an urgent issue and desperate for information, this can be infuriating. It will expedite your work if you understand the other agency's procedures and chain of command. By following their rules, you generally will get better service. Clearly identify yourself, your agency, and your request. Be prepared to show your credentials and have release-of-information forms available. Be patient while the other agency representative verifies your request and right to information. If a legitimate request is denied, you have two courses of action. You can ask to speak to a supervisor in that agency and try your request again, or you can go to your own supervisor for advice or intervention. As you gain experience, you will learn when to use which method. With the passage of time, you also will develop professional contacts with other agencies and know when it is appropriate to ask them to cut through red tape for you.

When you make a request of another agency that they cannot meet at the time, be sure to ask when the information will be ready. If you are working under a deadline, tell them. As you end your conversation, agree on a follow-up time. Something like, "I'll check back tomorrow after one if I don't hear from you sooner" is clear and gives the other agency time to work.

Limit discussions with other agency personnel to the probationer's case at hand. Some agency representatives may want to engage you in a discussion about other officers, the judges, or your chief. They may make complaints about other officers. Stay out of these discussions and refer any complaints to that officer's supervisor. Generally, you will not want to repeat such complaints to the other officer, but if they are serious, tell your own supervisor.

Criminal justice personnel change as do staff in other human service agencies. The child welfare worker who refused you information this week may be your coworker next month. Practice your best manners all the time to make the workplace more pleasant and productive.

TELEPHONE MANNERS

Professional people generally answer the phone with their first and last names. Your calls will have gone through a receptionist or automated answering system before they reach you, and if they were misrouted, you may have an irritated caller on the other end of the line. By clearly identifying yourself when you answer the phone, you avoid further confusion or wasted time, or you assure the callers that they have the right party. Something like "Sue Schmidt. May I help you?" is clear and professional. Likewise, when making calls, be sure to identify yourself and your agency at the beginning of the call. For example "This is John Jones from Smith County Adult Probation. May I speak to the judge, please?" If you are leaving a voice mail, be sure to state the date and time, your name and phone number (with area code, if appropriate). If your message is urgent, state your deadline. An example is the following: "This is Sue Schmidt at Smith County Adult Probation. It is 10:30, Tuesday morning, February 3rd. Please call me by noon today or we will have to pass on the Brown case. I'm at (703) 755-1234. Thanks."

Do not start talking without identifying yourself. Do not give information on incoming calls until you know the callers and whether they have a right to the information. Do not chew gum or eat while on the phone. It also is extremely irritating to have someone call you and put you on hold. Plan your outgoing calls to avoid this. If calls come in while you have an offender in your office, ask the callers if you may call them back after your office visit. Sometimes this is not possible. If the caller is asking for confidential information or opinions, excuse yourself long enough to escort your client to the waiting room and then finish the call.

In modern American society, there is an urgency about a ringing telephone that causes us to give phone calls priority over the presence of real, live people sitting in front of us. This is often rude and wrong. Take care not to get confused about what is more important. The key to good office etiquette is to remember that everyone wants respect. It is easier to get if you also give it.

KEY POINTS TO REMEMBER

The reader should be able to discuss each of the following items:

- Meet probationers in the lobby and escort them to your office.
- Decide on your approach to handshaking and be consistent.
- Use last names and titles.
- Do not allow any physical contact other than handshakes.
- Do not allow the probationer to close your door.
- Limit interruptions.
- Do not gossip or listen to complaints about other officers.
- Be careful about office romances.
- Use good manners with everyone.

Organization
and
Time Management

E verywhere in corrections, officers can be heard asking for extra help, smaller caseloads, training on time management, or just more hours in the day. It is true that workloads are heavy and difficult. The national average for regular probation is 117 (Camp and Camp, 1999). Even in juvenile probation and intensive supervision where caseloads traditionally have been smaller, the workload may be 50 or more per officer. All those probationers (3 ½ million according to Bureau of Justice 1998 statistics) have problems and needs to be addressed. Standards require certain paperwork be completed at specific times, and funding is tied to those deadlines.

Many officers are writing presentence investigations or other court reports, which are time consuming. Field visits take time. Hours can be lost sitting and waiting for a court appearance or seeing a probationer in jail. Juvenile officers may find themselves involved in lengthy school conferences or spending hours in the detention center or hospital emergency room. Someone is always absent due to illness, vacation, training, or other reasons, leaving their caseload to be picked up by other officers who already were busy. Urinalysis testing must be done and documented. Monthly statistics and collection reports are due. Collection letters and phone calls have to be made. Absconders have to be located. If your department is trying to convert to a new computer system, you may experience frustration as the kinks are discovered and worked out. There is always more to do than there is time in which to do it. Furthermore, this work is emotionally and mentally exhausting.

All these issues are true, and managers throughout corrections acknowledge the workload and the pressures involved. It is also true that employees everywhere (even in probation) waste time and could be organized better. Everyone has worked with the parent whose children are home alone after school and call repeatedly asking mom or dad to referee their fights. Office romances cost time and hurt department morale. Other personal phone calls and crises can have an adverse impact on the workplace. As on any job, there are officers who take extended smoke breaks, long lunches, or visit too much. Study the work patterns in your office for a week, including your own. Do a time study on yourself. Although there are days when you never slow down and you work right through lunch, there are also days with some "down" time. One important aspect of professionalism is self-management. Officers should monitor themselves and not have to be told by the administration that they are wasting time. The time you "find" can be put to productive use developing new programs, running groups, or supervising outside community service.

Scheduling Tools

We all need some structure to our workday or week. Even those with almost photographic memories can start missing deadlines and commitments with so much occurring. Some officers work in more than one location and have to travel great distances. Others may have additional duties, such as staff training, plus direct supervision of offenders. Do not trust your memory. Write everything down. Pick one place or method and write everything there. Get in the habit of doing business this way so that it becomes automatic. Remember, in this business, "If it isn't written down, it didn't happen." There are many different methods of scheduling. Investigate and choose the one that works best for your position and personal style.

CALENDARS

The most basic scheduling method is the calendar. Many officers work well from desk calendars. To use the calendar, follow these steps:

- Use only one calendar. Keep it on your desk and put everything on it. Additional art calendars on the wall may please your sense of aesthetics, but they also can lead to confusion. Sooner or later, someone (maybe even you) will write on these, and you will end up missing an appointment.

- Keep your calendar up to date. Check it first thing each morning and last thing before going home. Either check items off as they are completed, or move them to another day. When the month is over, tear off the page or pages and file them for future reference. They may contain information you will need later in court.

- Note on your calendar the date, time, and place of all meetings or appointments.

- Make a note on your calendar in advance of approaching deadlines. For instance, a presentence investigation (PSI) report is assigned to you on March 15, due March 30. Note on your calendar, the actual deadline (March 30-Smith PSI). Then, look at your schedule and note a day to begin (March 18-begin Smith PSI). Also, note on the calendar several days prior to the actual deadline as a reminder to review and deliver the report (March 27-deliver Smith PSI).

- If you are working on a long project or report that cannot be finished in one day, you will need to continue noting this on your calendar to be sure this assignment does not get lost in the confusion of day-to-day activities.

- Take care not to keep moving items to the next day without working on them. If this is occurring, you may have prioritized the item incorrectly or may not be realistic with your deadline.
- Note deadlines for others to provide you with information. For instance, you are waiting for urinalysis (UA) results for a hearing scheduled for December 10. Make a note on your calendar several days prior to the hearing to follow up on the test results (December 5-Jones UA due). This gives you time to get the information, even if others fail to follow through.

Daily Planners

Daily planners are similar to calendars but much more complex and provide tools for long-range planning and personal time management. Some of these (such as Priority Management) provide several days of training in time management and planning to accompany their material. If you decide to use a daily planner or organizer, make it your only scheduling tool. Keep it on your desk when you are in the office, and write everything in it. If you do business at home, take it with you.

The daily planners have space for telephone and fax numbers as well as addresses. They provide places for project planning and follow-up work. If you work in more than one location, these can become portable offices. Officers who have several different job duties also may find daily planners helpful in keeping their very different duties organized.

As with the calendar, do not keep moving items from one day to another. If your planner has a spot to prioritize items, be realistic about urgency and deadlines. Planners also may have a place for "call backs" or information due from other people. Be sure to note those deadlines also. If the party has not contacted you by the promised date, take action. For example, the police promise to deliver an offense report you need for court on July 5. They say it will be ready by July 2. You should have that date marked on your planner and you should call the police before the day is over if you do not receive the report. Remember, you are the one the court will be looking to for information, regardless of what the other agency does. As we suggested, check your planner every morning and the last thing every evening. You will be amazed and shocked at how much you can forget if you are relying on memory alone.

A word of warning about these portable offices: the addresses and phone numbers in your planner need to be kept secure. Probationers could access personal information about you or other officers from such books. Lock them up at the end of the day, or take them home with you.

ELECTRONIC DATEBOOKS/TICKLER SYSTEMS

You may prefer to keep all your appointments in an electronic date-book or similar system. The same principles apply as in calendars and daily planners: use only one tool, and put everything in it. Use deadlines and follow-up dates, check it at the beginning and end of each day. If you are continually moving an item from one date to the next, reassess its priority.

Electronic systems can be programmed to notify you if you have duplicated appointments. As with other methods, the key is to be consistent in making and checking entries. Have a back-up paper method in case of a system or power failure.

SCHEDULING APPOINTMENTS

The size and nature of the caseload as well as departmental policy will determine how often and when you see your probationers. Within those guidelines, most officers have great flexibility in scheduling. Failure to report is probably the most common probation violation. Although probationers will have excuses, these rarely will hold up to the reasonable man/woman standard. It is the officer's responsibility to establish reporting criteria at the first meeting with a probationer. Let the probationers know what the rules are, and tell them that you expect them to comply.

The last item of business at most office visits will be setting the next appointment. Once you and your probationer agree on a date and time, mark your calendar or reporting list and give the probationer an appointment card. Take your time doing this. Probationers will use any mistake you make as an excuse not to report next time. When setting appointments, be sure to allow for any scheduled time off, training, or court appearances. Do not schedule appointments when you know you will not be in the office. If this is absolutely necessary, be sure you have cleared this with the officer who will be substituting for you. Assuming that someone else will see your clients is bad for office morale. Probationers spot such weaknesses and use them to their own advantage. They will not be as cooperative with a substitute as they are with you, knowing the other officer is in a hurry to get back to his or her own probationers. Some probationers may fail to pay their fees or be unable to give a urinalysis sample if they think they can get away with this in your absence.

Allow adequate time for appointments. Most probationers present routine problems and can be seen quickly, if necessary, but everyone has some special cases that always take longer. If you know your caseload, you can schedule those very talkative probationers earlier in the day or you will still be listening at quitting time. For the sake of your own morale, you may want to schedule the very belligerent clients at times when you are at your best and better able to deal with them. Save certain time spots for probationers who have trouble getting off work or who have transportation problems and have to wait for a ride or the bus. Be sure to schedule time for your lunch and breaks. On really hectic days, this may be the only way you get out of the office.

Take into consideration when you are working at your peak. Many things are time driven and out of your control, but others can be scheduled according to your own preference. Most people are at their best in the middle to late morning, a little slow first thing in the morning and just after lunch, and are tired by the end of the day, but night owls start to peak in the late afternoon and early evening. See what your own body rhythms are, and plan your tasks accordingly.

Some departments have open reporting dates when all probationers must report during a specific period. For example, one county has everyone report by the tenth of the month. After that day, anyone who has not reported is in violation. If you work such a schedule, you probably will not want to plan any extra activities during reporting. Come to work rested, in comfortable shoes, have change for the soft drink machine, and bring your lunch. Childcare, grocery shopping, and other personal business should be under control beforehand as there will not be time once reporting starts.

In addition to your regular supervision duties, you need to allow adequate time for preparing reports, compiling monthly statistics, handling collections, training, and other duties. Try to block out an hour or so when you do not have appointments scheduled and you are not expected in court. If you have voice mail, you may want to have your calls routed to it while you do your reports, but try to return all messages the same day.

It is the probationer's responsibility to report—no one else's. This violation can result in a motion to revoke and incarceration. Although there are generally no good reasons for not reporting, there may be extenuating circumstances that make reporting difficult for many people. Transportation is one; work is another; childcare may be an issue, especially for women. Officers who know their caseload can prevent many problems and avoid setting the probationer up to fail by offering some scheduling options.

If your probationers travel by bus to report, be sure to give them a time when the buses are running. A woman with school age children may want to report after she has taken the children to school. Evening appointments are advantageous for many working people. If your department has late-night reporting, save these times for probationers who really need them. As we indicated earlier, if your department does not have late-night reporting, never agree to meet with a probationer after hours unless your supervisor has approved this and another officer will be with you. Although you may be perfectly willing to work late, it is dangerous to be alone with some probationers and the appearance of impropriety is also a possibility. Do not break office rules and put yourself in jeopardy in the process.

Track the reporting of your probationers and be ready to contact them as soon as they miss an appointment. You may use your calendar, a special reporting list, or an appointment book for this purpose. Your department probably has a method in place already. Whatever the method, follow up on all probationers every month. Never wait to see if they will report next time. This is tacit permission to miss appointments, and once allowed, most probationers will repeat this behavior. Let your probationers know that you accept no excuses for failure to report and that you will take quick action.

When probationers fail to report, make a note to contact them the next working day. If you can reach your probationers by telephone, schedule an office visit immediately. If you cannot reach them by phone, send a letter with a new appointment time. Allowing for mail service, a week from the date you send the letter is usually reasonable. Advise them that failure to report will result in further sanctions up to and including a motion to revoke. Keep a copy of this letter in the probationer's file for use if you end up in court.

If your probationer still does not respond, it is time for a field visit. You may find an abandoned house, or no one at home, but often a relative or roommate will be home. Leave your business card with a note for the probationer to call by the next working day. If there is still no response, it is time to file a violation report. Your department may handle these through administrative hearings or revocation hearings. Whatever the procedure, do not allow probationers to ignore reporting.

On occasion, you may find your probationer at home when you make the field visit. If this occurs, be careful about entering the house. You must consider the possibility that a probationer who refuses to report is under the influence of drugs or alcohol and could be dangerous. If there is any doubt in your mind, do not go inside. Give the probationers an appointment card and tell them it is imperative that they come in to the office. Some probationers are not dangerous at all, but they may be lazy about reporting. If this is the case and you do conduct a home visit, the probationer still should report to the office the next working day. Probationers making payments must do so in the office. If you notice something amiss during a home visit, it may be preferable to discuss this in the safety and quiet of your office. Finally, some probationers play power games with their officer in attempts to gain control. Allowing probationers to miss appointments takes away from the officer's authority and is "one up" for the probationer.

Field visits require some thought in scheduling to maximize time. Organize field visits by location to avoid excess driving. Consider your probationers' schedules so that you are not making field visits when you know they are not home. If you are working after dark, be sure you follow department policy for safety. These visits should be made in pairs. Take a cell phone and leave an itinerary.

Telephone and Time Management

Probation officers lose and waste a lot of time on phone calls to people who are not in, or on calls for which they do not have all the necessary information at hand. Much time is lost just listening to irate relatives of probationers. Although you must listen to these folks, there are some ways to use that time effectively. Some of these tips can save you time and aggravation:

- Never talk about a case without having the file in front of you. Talking to probationers "blind" may lead to off-the-cuff remarks that cause you trouble later. You are much more likely to give out incorrect information without the file. Furthermore, if you need to document the call, you are more likely to do so with it in front of you than if you have to pull it later.
- Do not place a lot of calls and leave messages just before leaving the office. This leads to phone tag and is mostly wasted effort.
- When you get stuck on the phone and you do not need to be taking notes, use that time to file. This used to be called "overlapping." Literally, it means you are overlapping one task with another.
- Return phone messages the day you get them. Refusing to return calls or procrastinating is not professional or polite. By making it a habit to return calls promptly, you gain a reputation as a responsible officer who can be counted on to call back. Failure to do so leads people to consider you lazy, arrogant, or afraid to talk to them, none of which is desirable.
- Limit your personal phone calls. This is a time waster and unfair to probationers and the taxpayer, as well.
- If your department has e-mail, you can eliminate many phone calls. E-mail is less intrusive and often delivers the same or more information than you would have gotten over the phone. You can make notes on your calendar or in the file and save paper, or print out your messages if you need a hard copy. Remember that e-mail is forever, so do not send anything that later would prove embarrassing.
- Use voice mail. The days of live receptionists are almost gone, and voice mail is often more reliable.
- Be sure you know who you are talking to when you are on the phone. If someone is asking for confidential information, ask for a

name and phone number where you can call back. This gives you a chance to assess if the individual really has a right to the information requested and allows you time to determine if they are who they claim to be. For example, a man calls identifying himself as a Secret Service agent. He says your probationer, John Brown, has threatened the President. Mr. Brown is capable of this, but you have never talked to the Secret Service before. Ask for a phone number, verify that it really is the Secret Service, and then call back. The agent will understand, and you will be covered.

- As a general rule, if a call with a probationer runs over five or ten minutes, you should consider scheduling a meeting. There are always exceptions, but long phone calls with probationers tend to leave problems unsolved. Save all that wasted phone time and schedule a meeting.

Paperwork: Not Necessarily a Dirty Word

Officers everywhere decry the flood of paperwork they have to process. The officer must fill out numerous forms. The officer also must process and file forms. The probationer's monthly report forms and financial reports must be read and filed. Statistical reports are due monthly. The paperwork continues. With the advent of the paperless workplace and computerized files, much of this someday may be eliminated. For now, however, most officers continue to juggle piles of paper.

The first and most basic tip regarding paperwork is do not shuffle paper. Pick it up, read it, process it, file it, or send it on to the next person. If you cannot process a piece of paperwork in one sitting, put it in a suspense file and mark your calendar for a date on which to work on it.

Filing can be done at a variety of times, including dead time during phone calls. If you have staff members who sit down and will not leave, you can file while they are taking up chair space. While waiting for an appointment to arrive, or at the end of the day preparing to go home, file.

MORE FILING

Your caseload will be filed alphabetically by the last name of the probationer. However, you have other kinds of files. Officers have files for forms, statistics, studies, reports, and professional reading. These files should be arranged alphabetically by topic or subject matter. Blank forms should be filed alphabetically. Remember to keep those frequently used forms in your desk or at arm's length. Report forms or chronological forms are good examples of forms you may want to keep in your desk. Remember, not only does orderly filing help you work faster and more efficiently, but other officers who cover your caseload can access files and forms better if you have organized things logically.

SUSPENSE FILES

The suspense file (also know as a tickler file) is a way for you to keep papers or documents that you cannot finish in one sitting and need to follow up on at a later date. Rather than rifle through all the papers on your desk, you may need to put such items in a holding place. A hanging file in your desk is ideal for this, but you may want to use a folder in a desk drawer, the in-box, or some other method. The important thing is to have a designated place for follow-up work and to note on your calendar with the date to follow up. Mark the document with the same date and get in the habit of checking your suspense file daily.

Items specific to a certain probationers' cases can be held in their file and the follow-up date noted on your calendar. However, when you are working on an assignment not unique to an individual probationer, such paperwork would go into the suspense file. For example, if you are working on the department's officer safety committee and you have a survey to mail out to officers due May 1, you would put a copy of the survey with its due date in your suspense file and mark your calendar on May 1, "surveys due." As they are returned to you, clip them together under the original copy. On May 1, you have a reminder on your calendar and all the information is in one place. Officers performing other jobs such as community service or training can benefit from a suspense file, and no supervisor should work without one.

TYPING AND PROOFING

For years, probation officers lost time correcting reports they had submitted for typing. With the computerization of most offices, you should be doing your own reports and eliminating this problem. If you have not already done so, learn how to do word processing. People who never could type well before can use the computer efficiently due to its delete key, spell check, easy margins, and other features. If you are using spell check, remember to check also for words that sound the same, but have different spelling and perhaps different meanings. Also, check for grammar. If you can do this with your document on the screen, you save time and paper. If you need a hard copy to proof, you still are saving time by doing it yourself rather than going through a typist, and if there are any errors, you will not be angry at your secretary.

Keep copies of everything you write pertaining to a specific case or policy. Documents related to an individual probationer should go into that client's file. File other documents according to topic or keep them in a correspondence/memo file, if appropriate. You may write something so good that you want your boss to see it or have it published. At some point, you may need to defend some action to another agency or department. Written documentation carries weight in court and elsewhere in business, so save your documentation. If you are storing all your documents in the computer, be sure you have a backup system, and transfer important work to a disk.

If someone else still types for you, read every word of every document. You do not want to put your name on any official report or correspondence with errors or that is sloppily done. If there are any errors, return the document to the typist for correction. Your name, not the secretary's, is on your reports, so your reputation is at stake. Politely, but firmly, return to the secretary and show the secretary any errors. For example: "Kathy, this should be advise, not advice. Can you get that corrected and back to me today? I need to deliver this to court in the morning. Thanks." Then, follow this up on your calendar or daily planner under information due from others. If you are getting errors from your clerical help, they need to know that their work is not satisfactory so they can improve.

A major reason for errors is the secretary's inability to read handwriting. If you are still using this system, try to write legibly and save everyone a lot of headaches. Remember, professional secretaries type exactly what they see. Do not expect someone else to correct your spelling or grammar. Have your material correct when you turn it in for typing.

GENERAL HOUSEKEEPING

Some people are pack rats and probation officers are no exception. When you receive mail or memos, read them and make a conscious decision about whether you need to save them. Most of the time, you do not. Memos notifying you of meetings can be destroyed once you note the date, time, and location on your calendar, but memos from the chief on policy and procedure need to be saved in a file created for this purpose. When your department gets a new phone list, destroy the old one instead of stapling the new one over it.

Make it a habit to eliminate as much paper as possible. If your department has e-mail, you often can read your mail, make any notations necessary on your calendar and delete the message without using any paper. This is faster and more ecologically sound than the standard copy for every staff member and extras for each bulletin board. As a rule, you do not need to save old copies of the criminal code, outdated department handbooks, and policy manuals. Toss these out with old phone books. Old information takes up valuable space and is sometimes confusing.

If you save every birthday card, thank you note, and other personal mail you receive, think about taking these home. If you choose not to do that, at least create one personal file where you stash such correspondence. Do not receive mail at work that you do not want others to see. Many departments have a practice of opening all incoming mail prior to distribution.

Plan your days and check your calendar before leaving the office each evening and again on arrival the next day. Organize phone calls and try to make these at times when the other party is likely to be in to avoid callbacks and "phone tag." Discourage friends and family from calling you at work; this is a major distraction and time waster in every workplace.

Key Points to Remember

The reader should be able to discuss each of the following items:

- Do a time management study on yourself.
- Use only one calendar, planner, and so forth.
- Check your scheduling tool first and last thing each day.
- Never see a probationer after hours without permission from your supervisor and another officer present.
- Explain reporting requirements at your first meeting with probationers and stick to them.
- Know your caseload.
- Document visits and calls as they happen.
- While holding or just listening on phone calls, do some filing.
- Return calls the day they are received; use e-mail and voice mail.
- Do not shuffle paper.

- Limit personal calls.
- Use a suspense file.

CHAPTER TEN

Stress *and* Burnout

There is a lot of talk in the criminal justice system about stress and burnout. When you begin your career, you may not be able to imagine that your job ever will seem dull or tedious. At some point, your supervisor or team partner will caution you about working too much overtime or getting too involved with your cases. You may discount these warnings as the talk of old, cynical, or lazy officers and tell your best friend that you will never be like that. And then, one day you will wake up wondering if that nagging headache is a good enough reason to miss work, or you will find yourself unable to go home at quitting time because you are too keyed up and want to meet the other officers for a beer, or you will fail to make a social services referral for one of your clients because it really does not matter anyway.

Welcome to burnout. All human services jobs are stressful and are noted for a high degree of employee burnout. Probation officers are prime candidates for this. *The Handbook on Probation Services/ Guidelines for Probation Practitioners and Management* (Klaus, 1998) has an excellent discussion on how the conflicting roles of custody and care exacerbate officer stress. Some departments protect their officers with good policy and procedures that alleviate unnecessary stress and provide guidelines that help staff deal with the unavoidable stressors. Unfortunately, many officers are on their own in this frequently discussed but poorly managed realm. The fact is that as professionals, officers carry individual responsibility for managing stress and avoiding burnout, but many do not know how. If your department or agency does not provide training on this topic, take the initiative to do some reading in professional publications and develop your own strategy.

The most obvious step in stress management and burnout prevention is to recognize that you are stressed. There are a number of self-tests appropriate for probation officers. In *Stressed Out* (1994), Gary Cornelius lists some signs for identifying burnout in corrections workers. Some of the common behaviors include the following:

- Exhaustion
- Apathy/lack of involvement with your job
- Bitterness
- Impatience
- Frequently calling in sick for the slightest reason
- Constant complaints

Even without a test, your friends, family, and coworkers probably will alert you if you are in danger. If your spouse complains that you bring the office home with you, if your best friend says you cannot talk about anything but work, if your supervisor cautions you, consider these red flags and take time to check yourself.

At the end of a busy day, it may be difficult to "come down" and leave the job behind. If you were angry or afraid during the day, these emotions and the strong physical reactions they evoke will take hours to subside. Probation officers sometimes endure verbal abuse at the hands of probationers, the public, or even other professionals. It is human nature to want to go home and "kick the dog." Officers can become personally involved with their casework to the point of being unable to detach at the end of the day. The best officers are balanced human beings who are sensitive to their probationers' needs and involved in their cases but not consumed by them. There are some basic steps you can take to protect yourself and extend the life and productivity of your career.

The Serenity Prayer teaches us to accept the things we cannot change, have the courage to change the things we can, and the wisdom to know the difference. This prayer is appropriate for probation officers. Early on, learn to separate what can be changed from what cannot, what responsibilities are yours and which are the offenders'. This very basic premise will help you in every aspect of life. Step one in stress prevention is to know the difference in what can be changed and what cannot.

The probationers you will supervise present an array of problems, needs, and risks, which can be overwhelming. Professional instruments are available to measure the individual offender's risk and need level. Yet, not all needs will be addressed—doing so is a human impossibility. All risks will not be detected and diverted. However, we can make intelligent and informed assessments and plan casework to allocate services. The use of such casework tools relieves the officer from many agonizing decisions and from accusations of discrimination or favoritism.

Step two in stress prevention is to use the approved tools and training provided by your agency. Officers need to be aware that some probationers will not change, regardless of the level of intervention. Others will change for the better, no matter what we do. The remaining offenders may or may not make positive changes depending on a number of factors. The officer/offender relationship is only one of the many influences in an offender's life. Officers need to learn how to walk the fine line between taking credit and avoiding responsibility. This requires more objectivity than many people possess, but it is a good goal. Part of professionalism is a commitment to deliver services to offenders fairly and without prejudice or bias. Officers committed to doing this will learn that even the most cynical sometimes can be pleasantly surprised at a probationer's success. If you are doing your job as you were trained, you do not need to take credit for successes (they really are the offenders'), and you do not need to take the blame for their failures. Step three in stress prevention is to take only the credit or responsibility due, and let the offender have the rest.

Every probation department has written and unwritten rules and procedures. These have been developed over time as a response to recurring problems or needs. By learning your department's procedures and following them, you can eliminate a lot of stress in your professional life. Officers who think they are smarter than the administration and who constantly spend time trying to circumvent the system make themselves and everyone else miserable. Following your department's chain of command and policy and procedures will expedite your workday, your career, and save a lot of wear and tear. Step four in stress prevention is to follow proper procedures. If these do not seem to work, review the appeal system in your agency or ask for individual cases to be staffed for referrals to other agencies more suited to handle the problem.

A major stressor for many new officers is allowing the job to become personal. Officers who are too impressed with their own authority can get into trouble this way and find themselves very anxious or angry. Remember, as an individual, you have no authority or influence. You are a servant of the court and the public. That spirit of servanthood can help save you from an overinflated sense of your own importance. When probationers fail to cooperate or become belligerent, when an attorney attacks your testimony on the witness stand, when the police do not call you back as promised, it is not a personal affront. Right or wrong, this is all a part of the day's work. Step number five in stress prevention is to separate your personal from your professional roles and reactions.

Messy and disorganized offices lend an air of messy and disorganized thinking. Although some people are superior performers even with a messy desk, many are not. Getting organized can help you work faster and more efficiently and eliminate unnecessary stress. Step six in stress prevention is to get your mind, your office, and your caseload organized.

Sometimes the volume of work and the hectic pace of our jobs cause us to get sloppy. You may find that you failed to document something or did not carry out a promised referral. When we allow ourselves to violate good work habits and disrupt routines, we fall victim to pressure and stress, which in turn, creates more stress. By following routine work habits (such as always documenting interactions with probationers as they occur) you can eliminate the stress of having to remember to do so. No one wants to wake up in the middle of the night wondering if they documented that appointment change or turned in a report on time. Step seven in stress prevention is to develop consistent work habits and follow them.

Busy people everywhere, not just probation officers, are trying to do too much and often sacrifice their own welfare in the process. All over the country, probation officers arrive at work early, skip lunch, and stay late every night. They congregate in the parking lot after work to smoke and maybe gripe. They never have enough time to see their children or run errands, and they rarely exercise or have quiet time. In a profession as demanding as probation, officers cannot afford to ignore their own needs.

Step eight in stress prevention is to take care of yourself. Carefully examine your need to be at the office ten hours a day. Either you are not managing your time well, you are overestimating your own indispensability, or you are avoiding going home. Start observing normal working hours and spend some of that "found" time taking care of yourself. Schedule time for exercise and for quiet time or meditation. Make special time for your spouse or children. Set up standing appointments with your best friend for movies or dinner. Enroll in a course just for fun. Get at least eight hours sleep per night and revisit the basic food groups. You are more than just a probation officer, and you need to develop the rest of your life in order to stay healthy and viable.

Some people are afraid of failure, so they never try anything and never fail. Failure is a bad word in our society, but it is not a totally negative thing. Many times it is a way to learn. Do not be afraid to try for fear of failure. The process itself is a learning experience and will expand your mind and sometimes your heart. Human beings overcome fear by doing the thing they are afraid of. Step nine in stress prevention is to face your fears and take action.

Probation is a serious business. Officers ought to take seriously their oath and the impact they have on people's lives. At the same time, we are human and so is our clientele. Most things are not irreparable. Many things we see and hear are funny. When you can, lighten up. Smile more. Say a pleasant word whenever you can. Focus on what is good, true, and uplifting instead of what is negative. Step ten in stress prevention is not to take yourself too seriously.

By identifying your own risk level and taking steps all through your career to prevent or eliminate stress, you can avoid much of the risk of burnout. If you find yourself bottomed out anyway, seek the advice of a trusted officer or supervisor for a fresh perspective. Seek out training to address your need. Brainstorm for new ideas and methods to approach casework that will be good for you and your probationers. Review your department's mission and philosophy, and spend time in professional reading. Consider asking for a different type of caseload or different job duties.

If you have done all this and still feel burned out and washed up, seek professional help. Most agencies provide employee assistance programs and/or health insurance that covers mental health issues. Burnout may be a signal of much deeper depression, which requires professional intervention.

It is possible for some people to burn out and come back. For others, burnout may mean they need to look at a career move. To consider spending twenty to thirty years in probation may be too much to ask of some people. This is not a weakness. Holding on just until retirement is a disservice to the court, the public, the probationers, and most of all, to yourself. Many good officers are lost or rendered ineffective because they ignored the warning signs of stress and impending burnout. Take the offensive and do not let this happen to you.

KEY POINTS TO REMEMBER

The reader should be able to discuss each of the following items:

- Stress and burnout are preventable.
- Burnout is easier to prevent than cure.
- Evaluate yourself for risk.
- Practice the Serenity Prayer.
- Get organized.
- Take care of yourself.
- Follow approved procedures.
- Separate the personal from the professional.

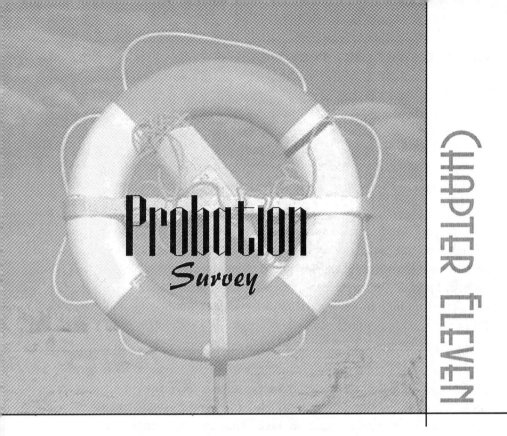

Probation
Survey

For the writing of this book, the membership of the National Association of Probation Executives who had e-mail was surveyed about the qualities and training they look for in probation officer candidates. Four questions were posed to these 100 people:

1. What are the two or three most important qualities you look for in the successful candidate for a position of probation officer?
2. What two or three things do you most want new officers to know about how to supervise offenders?
3. What training, education, and life experience would you most like criminal justice students to have before they enter the workplace?
4. What should people planning a career in probation know about that career choice?

The response was swift and enthusiastic. Many sent additional information and materials along with the surveys. Their advice to students and those considering a probation career is presented here with gratitude and the hope that readers take note. What follows is the voice of a millennium's worth of experience.

Participants named good communication skills, both verbal and written, more often than any other quality (54 percent). They said that they look for people with good skills who can communicate effectively with a variety of people and agencies. Cultural diversity issues and philosophical differences help to make clear communication increasingly difficult. Those with good communication skills are prized candidates.

Integrity, honesty, and character were listed by 29 percent of those responding. An additional 4 percent named loyalty, commitment, and courage—qualities closely related to the character issue. Tied with integrity was organizational ability. Chiefs look for people who can organize, prioritize, and manage multiple tasks. One executive added that he looks for people who are goal oriented.

The third most frequently named quality was that of interpersonal skills (25 percent). Probation officers must like people and be able to get along with a wide variety of them. This is closely related to having a cooperative attitude, which was the fifth most frequently named quality at 14 percent. Officers must like people, enjoy working with them, and recognize that due to the diversity among probationers and officers, they will need to be flexible. Flexibility was named by 21 percent of the executives. They cite a need for officers who can learn different coping mechanisms and approaches to deal with the many different responsibilities and people they encounter.

They also want new officers to understand that there are many different philosophies about probation, and the current "rethinking" debate may influence change in the way we carry out duties in the future. Officers must be able to adapt, be creative, and use many different styles and skills to be effective. Another 21 percent rated intelligence or the ability to learn as very important. As one respondent said, officers should be "trainable;" another calls this "moldable."

In addition to the top five qualities named, respondents discussed the importance of a good sense of humor, common sense, patience, the desire to help people without being judgmental, enthusiasm, and cultural sensitivity. One executive looks for diverse qualities in the candidates for probation officer to see what unique thing each can bring to the workplace. Just mentioned in passing were also such characteristics as physical and mental stamina, respect for the law, creativity, and a basic understanding of who probation clients are.

Responding to the second question of what new officers need to know about how to supervise offenders, the overwhelming answer was the necessity of being consistent and "fair but firm." Twenty-nine percent named this. Just behind this at 25 percent was the need to treat all people with dignity and respect. Many people added comments about remembering that we deal with human beings who have unique needs. Officers need to know that a variety of styles, techniques, and approaches will be necessary to supervise offenders (21 percent). Although newly hired officers cannot be expected to have developed such variety, they do need to understand its importance and be willing to develop such skills and tools.

Public safety was a concern for 17 percent of the respondents. Executives want officers to understand their duty to the public for protection and be able to put this before other obligations. Another 14 percent talked about danger to the individual officer and want officers to be able to understand and recognize it.

In response to question three regarding the best education, training, and life experiences for students prior to entering the workplace, a resounding 46 percent named internships as the most valuable thing one can do in preparation for a probation career. Internships were valued for providing "reality checks" for students as well as for their instructive nature. Another 21 percent named volunteer work in corrections or with similar populations as highly desirable. The feeling was that the more contact students have with probationers and similar populations, the more reliable their career decisions can be.

Although most jurisdictions require a minimum of a bachelor's degree to be hired, and 28 percent of respondents listed this, there was more discussion and emphasis on the internship than anything else. Regarding formal education, respondents differed in preference for criminal justice or other behavioral science degrees as opposed to a variety of courses and areas of interest. Many listed English or Spanish (17 percent), computer science (17 percent) along with business, and history as desirable majors. The executives were interested in hiring balanced, well-rounded individuals whose world view would be broad enough to cope with the reality of probation.

Twenty-five per cent said that actual work experience (any job at all in some cases) was desirable, and 17 percent said that experience with similar populations was important. Especially good work experience includes military duty, previous law enforcement or corrections employment, substance abuse work, and jobs with high interpersonal contact and opportunity for conflict.

Finally, regarding the last question of what people planning a probation career should know, 42 percent said that prospective officers should know that this work is intrinsically rewarding, but you "can't get rich." Low pay or pay not equal to the educational requirements and responsibilities was named by 39 percent. The work is challenging and the field is constantly changing according to 14 percent. Another 14 percent add that the work is hard and stressful. Paperwork is a major issue for probation personnel and these executives are well aware of its impact. Ten percent named this as important to know in advance.

Also mentioned were the opportunity to be creative the vast discretion allowed most officers in decision making and casework issues. Several executives stated that the work is important and has an impact on all of society. Others talked about the need to stay positive and not become cynical in the face of offender failures. "The fellowship of other officers" and the need for "heart" were also concerns. Some good advice from Ted Hanchett, Chief Probation Officer for the 17th Judicial District of Kansas, is that small jurisdictions allow more experience than larger ones because in small jurisdictions, the officer does everything.

One of the most significant things about this survey was how positive most of the answers were. There were only a few negatives named, and these only as realistic necessities. An enormous sense of pride and accomplishment came through in almost every response. We are an important link in the criminal justice system. We supervise more offenders than anyone else in the system. Our ability to change and grow with the challenges of the future is unrivaled by any other segment of criminal justice. Our roots in social work make us uniquely qualified for implementing true community corrections and restorative justice measures. We are a professional community dedicated to the public safety and individual rehabilitation of offenders, and we believe that the two are not mutually exclusive.

In closing, let's look at a quote from David Carlson, editor of *Jubilee* magazine:

"Ultimately restorative justice comes from God Himself . . . a justice that calls for accountability, repentance, forgiveness and restoration." *Herein lies the heart of probation.*

REFERENCES

Allen, Bud and D. Bosta. 1981. *Games Criminals Play*. Sacramento, California: Rae John Publishers. Available from the American Correctional Association, Lanham, Maryland.

American Correctional Association. 1998. *1998-2000 Probation and Parole Directory*. Lanham, Maryland, American Correctional Association.

Arola, T. and R. Lawrence. 1999. Broken windows probation the next step in fighting crime. *Perspectives*. August. American Probation and Parole Association.

Basile, Vincent. 1995. Restorative justice and the balanced approach. *Executive Exchange*. Fall.

Bennis, Warren. 1989. *On Becoming a Leader*. Reading, Massachusetts: Addison-Wesley Publishing Company.

Bureau of Justice Statistics. August, 1999. *Bulletin*. Washington, D.C.: U.S. Department of Justice.

Bush, Jay, B. Glick, and J. Taymans. 1997. *Thinking for a Change: Integrated Cognitive Behavior Change Program.* Longmont, Colorado: National Institute of Correctons.

Camp, C. and G. Camp. 1998. *Corrections Yearbook 1998.* Middletown, Connecticut: Criminal Justice Institute, Inc.

Carlson, David. Winter, 2000. *Jubilee.* Washington, D.C.: Prison Fellowship Ministries.

Cohn, Alvin, Ed. 1994. *Field Officer's Resource Guide.* Laurel, Maryland: American Correctional Association.

Cornelius, Gary. 1994. *Stressed Out.* Laurel, Maryland: American Correctional Association.

Cox, Brian, Judy Burd, and Ed Roberts. 1997. *Cognitive Intervention.* Huntsville, Texas: Windham School District.

Donohue, William A. and Robert Kolt. 1992. *Interpersonal Conflict.* Newbury Park, California: Sage Publications, Inc.

Dunlap, Karen, Ed. 1998. *Community Justice Concepts and Strategies.* Lexington, Kentucky: American Probation and Parole Association.

Evans, Donald. 1999. Broken windows fixing probation. *Corrections Today.* December. American Correctional Association.

Federal Judicial Center. 1993. *Officer Safety: Strategies For Survival.* Washington, D.C.: Court Education Division.

Fox, Grace. 1996. *Everyday Etiquette.* New York: Guild America Books.

Harvey, Eric and Alexander Lucia. 1994. *144 Ways to Walk the Talk.* Dallas, Texas: The Walk the Talk Company.

Henningsen, Rodney, Dan Beto, Toby Ross, and David Bachrach. 1999. The probationer as a customer a Texas survey. *Texas Probation Journal.* (11)1.

Johnson, Herbert. 1980. *History of Criminal Justice.* Cincinnati, Ohio: Anderson Publishing.

Klaus, John F. 1998. *Handbook on Probation Services/Guidelines for Probation Practitioners and Management.* United Nations Publication.

Lasater, Richard. 1995. Victim awareness in adult community supervision. *Executive Exchange.* Fall.

Latessa, Edward, editor 1999. *Strategic Solutions: The International Community Corrections Association Examines Substance Abuse.* Lanham, Maryland: American Correctional Association.

Little, Gregory and Robinson, Kenneth. 1997. *Understanding and Treating Antisocial Personality Disorder: Criminals, Chemical Abusers and Batterers.* Memphis, Tennessee: Eagle Wing Books.

Lum, Doman. 1996. *Social Work Practice and People of Color.* Pacific Grove, California: Brooks/Cole Publishing Co.

National Institute of Justice. February, 1999. *Casework Management in the Criminal Justice System.* Washington, D.C.: National Institute of Justice.

Nidorf, Gary. 1996. Probation and parole officers or social workers? *Correctional Issues: Community Corrections.* Lanham, Maryland: American Correctional Association.

Orlandi, Mario. 1995. *Cultural Competence for Evaluators.* Washington, D.C.: U.S. Department of Health and Human Services.

Parole and Probation Officers. 1995. *Corrections Compendium*. February. Cega Services.

Parsonage, W., and J. Miller. 1993. *Officer Safety: Strategies for Survival*. Washington, D.C.: U.S. Department of Justice.

Probation Officers: Cops or Counselors. 1995. *Corrections Compendium*. February. Cega Services.

Pursley, Robert. 1977. *Introduction to Criminal Justice*. Encino, California: Glencoe Publishing Company, Inc.

Radelet, Louis. 1986. *Police and the Community*. New York: Macmillan Publishing Co.

Ramirez, Manuel III. 1999. *Multicultural Psychotherapy*. Needham Heights, Massachusetts: Allyn and Bacon.

Sowell, Thomas. 1981. *Ethnic America*. Boulder, Colorado: Basic Books.

Tannen, Deborah. 1990. *You Just Don't Understand*. New York: Ballantine Books.

Texas Department of Criminal Justice/Community Justice Assistance Division. 1990. *Working with the Difficult Probationer*. Austin, Texas: Texas Department of Criminal Justice.

University of Washington. News release. February, 17, 1999.

Walsh, Anthony. 1997. *Correctional Assessment, Casework and Counseling, 2nd Edition*. Lanham, Maryland: American Correctional Association.

About the Author

Earlene Festervan is a Summa Cum Laude graduate of Stephen F. Austin State University and holds a master's degree in criminal justice management from Sam Houston State University. She has worked in community corrections since 1984, in both juvenile probation and parole, as well as adult probation. Since 1992, she has served in several capacities as an assistant director for Jefferson County Residential Services. She currently supervises the first and only all-female restitution center in Texas. This facility has been recognized by the National Crime Prevention Council and the Texas Association for Residential Service Providers for its record-breaking restitution payments to victims and for low recidivism rates since its inception in 1997. Ms. Festervan has extensive experience as a trainer and public speaker and has written a number of programs for both employees and probationers. She is an avid gardener and a devotee of convertible riding and rhythm and blues music.